PHOTOSHOP FOR THE WEB

PHOTOSHOP FOR THE WEB

Mikkel Aaland

O'REILLY™

Cambridge · Köln · Paris · Sebastopol · Tokyo

Photoshop for the Web
by Mikkel Aaland

Copyright © 1998 Mikkel Aaland. All rights reserved.
Printed in the United States of America.

Editor: Richard Koman
Production Editor: Nicole Gipson Arigo

Printing History:

April 1998:   First Edition.

This book is printed on acid-free paper with 85% recycled content, 15% post-consumer waste. O'Reilly & Associates is committed to using paper with the highest recycled content available consistent with high quality.

ISBN: 1-56592-350-2

CONTENTS

PREFACE

Many books have been written on Adobe Photoshop, but until now none have focused specifically on using Photoshop for web production: this one does. In *Photoshop for the Web,* you'll learn all about GIFs and JPEGs, and how to use Photoshop to create web graphics that look great and download quickly. You'll learn step-by-step techniques for creating web type, navigational devices, and backgrounds. You'll even learn the best way to convert vector graphics to bitmap and how to use Photoshop as a web layout tool.

Photoshop for the Web draws on my 9 years in new media production and 24 years as a professional photographer, as well as the generous advice and wisdom of 25 full-time web producers whose tips and techniques grace the book. It's my hope that you'll find each chapter literally bursting with new and relevant information.

What you need to know

This is by no means a basic Photoshop book. Nor is it a comprehensive guide. In order to get the most out of the information provided here, you should have a working knowledge of at least Photoshop 3.0. While you don't need to use Photoshop 4.0 to create web graphics, I do recommend it. As you'll see throughout the book, this release makes web designers' lives easier in a number of ways. If you haven't upgraded yet, don't worry. Where Photoshop 4.0-specific techniques are discussed, I also include ways to do the same thing in Photoshop 3.0.

For more comprehensive guides to Photoshop, I recommend *Photoshop in a Nutshell* by Donnie O'Quinn and Matt LeClair (O'Reilly & Associates) and *The Photoshop Wow! Book* by Linnea Dayton and Jack Davis (Peachpit Press). If you're interested in the inner workings of graphic file formats, try *The Encyclopedia of Graphic File Formats* by James D. Murray and William vanRyper (O'Reilly).

How this book is organized

This book falls loosely into three main areas of organization. The first two chapters deal with general issues of image processing for the Web. Chapter 1, *Making Photoshop Web-Friendly,* explains how to set up Photoshop to accommodate the rules of the Web. Chapter 2, *Improving Photos for the Web,* focuses on preparing and optimizing photographs and other continuous-tone art for the Web.

The next section covers in detail the the Web's two most important graphic file formats, GIF and JPEG, Chapter 3, *Making Great GIFs,* and Chapter 4, *Creating GIFs from Scratch,* show how to convert existing graphics to GIF and how to create browser-safe GIFs from scratch. Chapter 5, *Special Effects with Transparent GIFs,* explains the ins and outs of transparency, including how to avoid the dreaded halo effect. Chapter 6, *JPEG: All the Color You Want,* gives you the low-down on JPEG, the 24-bit format of choice for photographs.

The next three chapters give step-by-step instructions for creating backgrounds (Chapter 7, *Creating Background Tiles*), graphical type (Chapter 8, *Photoshop Web Type*), and navigational devices (Chapter 9, *Creating Navigational Graphics*). Chapter 10, *Importing Vectors into Photoshop,* shows you how to avoid some of the pitfalls that are associated with importing Adobe Illustrator and Macromedia Free-Hand vector-based files into Photoshop. Finally, Chapter 11, *Laying Out Pages in Photoshop,* goes into great detail describing how Photoshop is used by web producers as the web design tool of choice.

In the appendices, you'll find information on PNG, a new file format that is gaining widespread support, as well as more details on useful Photoshop plug-ins and filters that extend the capabilities of Photoshop. You'll also find more information on the contributors featured in this book.

Photoshop and animation

Most of the techniques in this book will be useful for the web producer with animation in mind. Animation, after all, consists of a sequence of images or graphics that must be either created or prepared for the Web—with pretty much the same limitations of any single image destined for the Web. If you are interested in specific information pertaining to animation programs, O'Reilly has two useful books that I highly recommend: *GIF Animation Studio* by Richard Koman and *Shockwave Studio* by Bob Schmitt.

A reminder on copyright

As you'll see throughout this book, it is very easy to download and "borrow" images and graphics from the Web. With Photoshop it is tempting to incorporate others' work into your own. I just want to remind you that much of the material that you see on the Web is copyrighted. Behind most images and graphics is a person, company, or institution that owns and controls the copyright to that image. It's one thing to download an image or graphic from the Web for personal use, and quite another to possess the legal rights to actually use the image for one of your own projects.

The law is very clear: if you use a copyrighted image without permission, statutory damages can be assessed against you and copies of the infringing work can be ordered destroyed. If you have any doubts about your rights to use work you find on the Web, especially if your work is commercial, don't take chances. Either contact the artist directly to request permission or consult a legal expert.

What's in Photoshop's future?

Although Adobe has been supportive of this book, they haven't given us any inside information about what to expect with subsequent versions of Photoshop. With Version 4.0, however, Adobe showed that they know which way the wind is blowing by including a Web palette as well as PNG and Progressive JPEG support. Clearly, in time, Photoshop will become even more web-friendly.

What would web designers like to see in subsequent versions? Here is my list:

- A real-time view of the effects of different JPEG compression settings with corresponding file size information. (Plug-ins such as Pro-JPEG and HVS JPEG already offer this feature.)

- A faster way to toggle between indexed and RGB mode.

- An easy way to apply dithering selectively (I've featured a workaround in Chapter 3).

- A way to import Illustrator files into Photoshop with Illustrator layers intact (I've included a workaround in Chapter 10).

photoshop.webreview.com

In order to keep the price of this book as low as possible, we've opted to print most of the book in black and white, with a color insert for the images for which color is most important. Color figures have a prefix of C, as in Figure C-1. To see all of the images printed here in color, visit the official web site for this book at *photo-shop.webreview.com*. In addition to those images, the site will include new information about Photoshop, plug-ins, useful actions, and news and reviews about the book. If you have additional tips or information you'd like to share, please visit the site and contribute.

Platform differences

Photoshop works similarly on Macintosh and Windows. The only important difference for our purposes is the use of modifier keys. When you use the Command key on the Mac, you use the Control key on Windows. When you use the Option key on the Mac, you use the Alt key on Windows. In this book, we've indicated both modifer keys together. So where we say Command/Control, you should press Command if you're using a Mac and Control if you're using a Windows PC, and likewise for Option/Alt.

Acknowledgments

This book grew out of a lunch with Richard Koman, the editor of this book. He said two words: "Photoshop" and "Web," and I was hooked. During the next year, Richard gave me his full support, as we shaped, molded, and otherwise brought his good idea to life.

I'd also like to thank David Rogelberg, my agent, for introducing me to the fine folks at O'Reilly, and for giving me wise counsel throughout this project.

Thanks to Beverly Scherf, who kept insisting that the material in this book be not only accurate but understandable and who encouraged me at the lowest moments, and to Michael Foldes for his Windows expertise.

I'd also like to thank Michael Rogers, Newsweek Interactive; Ken Phipps; Paula Savage, Savage Design; Doug Frohman, Digital Frontiers; Marsha Weiner; Paul Foldes; Jessica Gould, CorelDRAW!; Heather Dittmer, BoxTop Software; Heather Heller, Heller Information Services; Russell Brown, Adobe Systems; Dennis Poon, IDEO; Fredrick Helmstrand, Icon Media Lab; Andrea Jenkins, Microsoft Sidewalk; Chris Vail, New Century Network; Kristin Keyes; Fred Shippey; Laurie McEachron, PhotoDisc; Kevin Connor, Adobe; John Leddy, Adobe; Sonya Schaefer, Adobe; Lori Barra, TonBo designs; Mark Holmes, National Geographic Online; Fred Sotherland, c|net; Ellen McNeilly; Susan Klemens, Discovery Channel Online; David Spitzler, Adobe; Taylor, HotWired; Cotton Coulson, c|net; Scott Highton; Rudy Burger; Susan Dunsworth; Jennifer R. Melnick; Julie Coburn, SFGate; John Caserta, *Chicago Tribune*; Edie Freedman, O'Reilly &

Associates; Dan Marcolina, Marcolina Design; Graham Hamilton; Donna Mann; Valerie May, National Geographic Online; Jim Irvine, SFGate; Alice Kreit, Washington Post.com; Sherry Rogelberg, Studio B; Michael Borek; John Nay, AAA; Lisa Waltuch, Discovery Online; Gary Hokke, PhotoDisc; Mary Anne Koopman, Newsweek Interactive; Sam Merrill, Photo District News; Anders Ottosson, Icon Media Lab; and Diana Rathe.

Many thanks also to the designers and web producers who contributed their valuable tips and techniques to this book. Their willingness to share is largely what made this book possible. (In Appendix C, *Contributor Notes*, you'll find them individually noted with a short bio and an email address.) I'd especially like to thank Valerie Stambaugh, a talented designer in Washington, D.C. with a heart of gold; Sean Parker of ParkerGrove; Brian Frick of MSNBC; and Gregg Hartling of Venu Interactive.

Thanks to all the people at O'Reilly & Associates. Richard Koman was the content editor. Nicole Gipson Arigo was the production editor and project manager. Jane Ellin copyedited the book, Nancy Wolfe Kotary proofread the book, and Claire Cloutier LeBlanc and Sheryl Avruch performed quality control checks. Madeleine Newell and Will Plummer provided production assistance. Nancy Priest designed both the interior format of the book and the layout for the color insert. Edie Freedman designed the cover. Gerry Azzata and Seth Maislin wrote the index. Mike Sierra implemented the format in Framemaker 5.0. Robert Romano edited the illustrations in Photoshop 4.0.

Finally, I want to thank my wife, Rebecca Taggart, who not only gave me encouragement and moral support, but applied her immeasurable skills as a writer/editor to the manuscript as well.

—Mikkel Aaland
San Francisco, 1998

CHAPTER ONE

MAKING PHOTOSHOP WEB-FRIENDLY

Photoshop has long been the image manipulation and processing tool of choice for photographers, designers, printing prepress operators, fine and commercial artists, multimedia designers, and many others. Photoshop is also the tool of choice for those of us designing web pages and creating images for the Web.

But while the program is a fantastic tool for web designers, it's set up for print, not for the Web. The first step in using Photoshop as a web design tool is to prepare it for web work. This includes customizing preferences to reflect the needs of the Web, opening a browser-safe swatch palette, and calibrating the display monitor to establish some sort of objective reference for viewing work.

Stop wasting bytes

Creating images for the Web is a constant struggle to reduce file size. Because the Web is a bandwidth-challenged place, and because we're competing with thousands of other sites for audience, it's crucially important to minimize graphics' file size. The last thing you want to do is to waste bytes. But that's what happens if you accept Photoshop's default preferences. In this section, you'll learn how to shrink your files by changing Photoshop's default preferences.

Turn off image previews

Unless you change your preferences, Photoshop always creates an icon and thumbnail version of your image when you save an image. This makes it convenient to identify images from your desktop or a dialog box; however, it increases the overall image file size anywhere from a few kilobytes to 30% of the file's size.

In this chapter

- Stop wasting bytes
- Other web-friendly preferences
- Creating a browser-safe swatch
- Using Actions for web production
- Calibrating your monitor
- Take the time

To turn off image previews in Photoshop 4.0, select File: Preferences: Saving Files. In Photoshop 3.0, the relevant dialog is located at File: Preferences: General: More.

Whichever version you're using, you'll see options at the bottom of the dialog box for Image Previews and Thumbnails, as shown in Figure 1-1. You can choose between Never Save, Always Save, and Ask When Saving. When you choose Ask When Saving, the Save, Save As, and Save a Copy dialogs let you choose whether to save the icon and thumbnail previews. The Ask When Saving option gives you flexibility, but can be a pain if you're working primarily on web images.

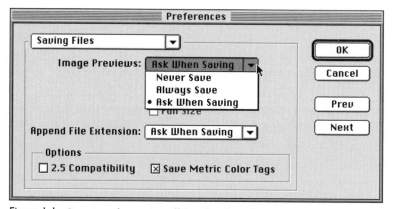

Figure 1-1. *Save space by turning off thumbnails and image previews*

Turning off image previews may or may not dramatically affect the size of your files. It depends on how you plan to use the image, what computer platform you are working with, and what format you've saved your work in.

For instance, when you upload a GIF file to a web server, the process actually strips all extraneous data—including thumbnails—from the file. So, there's no harm in taking advantage of the convenience of previews and thumbnails when working on GIF files for the Web.

It's a different story when creating JPEGs on a Macintosh. In this case, uploading the file doesn't strip extraneous data, so there is always a penalty of a few kilobytes if you leave previews and thumbnails on. If you're using a PC, though, don't worry about it; extraneous data will be stripped.

If you happen to process your images through Equilibrium Debabelizer, you're off the hook, because Debabelizer takes care of stripping out the preview data.

Many web designers maintain that it's good practice to turn off thumbnails and icons regardless of how much space can be saved. Not only does this save hard drive space, but it also speeds up the transmission of images as you send these files around a work environment and upload them to servers. You can always compensate for not having a visual representation of the image by descriptively naming your files.

Turn off 2.5 compatibility

Photoshop 3.0 marked the appearance of layers, probably the most popular enhancement to the program. The addition of layers resulted in a new file format, one that couldn't be read by the baseline version, Photoshop 2.5. (Adobe rewrote the software from the ground up for Version 2.5.), 2.5 is the Photoshop format supported by other programs like Adobe PageMaker and Debabelizer. So, in Photoshop 3.0 and later, Photoshop files can be 2.5-compatible, which is the default setting. To accomplish this, Photoshop actually creates an entirely new file that contains a layer-flattened version of your image.

By turning off 2.5 compatibility, you can significantly reduce your file size, which is especially important if you are sending files between workplaces or want to save hard disk space. This option affects only Photoshop files, not GIFs or JPEGs, so leaving it on doesn't affect the size of your web images. The option is found in Photoshop 4.0 under File: Preferences: Saving Files, and in Photoshop 3.0 under File: General: More.

Avoid unwanted colors

When you resize or transform an image in Photoshop, it uses one of three complex mathematical formulae to carry out the task: *Bicubic* (the default setting), *Bilinear*, or *Nearest Neighbor*.

- *Bicubic* is the most complex and therefore time-consuming method. It actually analyzes all the data inside and outside the area to be resized or transformed and then "intelligently" adds pixels and color values when needed. (It is also the default method.)

- *Bilinear* is similar to Bicubic, but analyzes data from a smaller sampling area before adding color values. This method is less accurate but faster than Bicubic. In practice, Bilinear is rarely used.

- *Nearest Neighbor* doesn't use any intelligent guessing to determine what colors should be added or subtracted when an image is resized or transformed. As the name implies, it looks to the

---

A word about Debabelizer

Debabelizer will open a Photoshop 3.0 or higher file *only* if the 2.5 option is turned off *and* the layers of the image have been flattened.

nearest pixel for color information, never adding color data that isn't already present in the image.

Most people use Bicubic, because it results in the highest quality by actually adding data when needed. But this is not always the best method for web production. For example, say you have a graphic that you have carefully indexed and applied specific, browser-safe colors to. You save it as a GIF, and later want to touch it up or add a specific detail. You open it in Photoshop and convert it to RGB mode. Now, because of the way the Bicubic algorithm interpolates data, if you even slightly transform or resize the image, you'll be inadvertently adding new—and probably unwanted—colors to the graphic and increasing its file size.

To avoid this, you might consider changing your preference to Nearest Neighbor. This is the least precise and fastest form of interpolation, but because this method doesn't introduce new colors to an image, it is sometimes the most desirable. A major drawback to this method is that it often creates jagged edges; in some cases, such as a small graphic, this may not be noticeable. Although the quality is lower with Nearest Neighbor, you can sometimes improve it by applying the Unsharp Mask filter when you are finished.

To change the way that Photoshop interpolates data and possibly save kilobytes, choose File: Preferences: General, as shown in Figure 1-2. In Photoshop 4.0, when you choose Image: Image Size, you are also given a choice of interpolation methods.

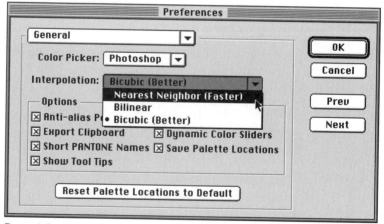

Figure 1-2. *Avoid color contamination and larger file sizes by choosing Nearest Neighbor*

Other web-friendly preferences

Here are some Photoshop preferences that won't result in a smaller file size but will save you time and make Photoshop more web-friendly.

You must use the proper file extension when you save a file to use on the Web. For example, JPEG files must end in .jpg or .jpeg, GIF files must end in .gif, and PNG files must end in .png.

Photoshop 4.0 for the Mac can automatically add the appropriate extension to the filename, as shown in Figure 1-3. (This is not an option in Windows because Windows requires all files to have extensions.) Unfortunately, Photoshop adds these extensions in capital letters, an unrecognizable format for some Unix servers, so you'll have to change the suffix to lowercase. Since you'll have to retype the extension anyway, and you may already be in the habit of adding file extensions, this option is probably more of an irritant than a time-saver.

To set the file extension option in Photoshop 4.0 for the Mac, select File: Preferences: Saving Files. Look for the Append File Extension option and select Never, Always, or Ask When Saving.

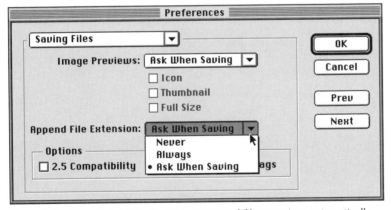

Figure 1-3. *Photoshop 4.0 for the Mac can append file extensions automatically*

You can also command Photoshop to add an extension when you select a format from the Save or Save As dialog by simultaneously pressing the Option/Alt key when you select a file format.

Units and rulers

Pixels matter in the bitmap world of the Web, so it's a good idea to set your Units & Rulers preference to pixels rather than inches, picas, or centimeters. (Since screen resolution is 72 pixels per inch and there are 72 points to an inch, either *pixels* or *points* are acceptable.)

To change your measurement units, choose File: Preferences: Units & Rulers (File: Preferences: Units in Photoshop 3.0) and change the Rulers setting to pixels (or points), as shown in Figure 1-4. You can also bring up this dialog by double-clicking on the rulers in your Photoshop window.

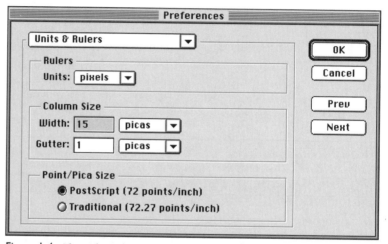

Figure 1-4. *The Web is a bitmap world, so set your units to pixels*

Alternatively, you can change your preferences by following these steps:

1. Display the Info palette.

2. Click and hold the icon to the left of the *XY* field.

3. Select a unit from the drop-down menu.

Guides and grids

Many web designers are using Photoshop as a layout tool, now that Photoshop 4.0 includes guides and grids, as shown in Figure 1-5. It's easier than ever to align type, graphics, and images with a web page in mind. The Guides and Grid preference found under File: Preferences: Guides & Grid allows you to control the colors, width, and frequency of the guides and grid lines. See Chapter 11, *Laying Out Pages in Photoshop*, for more information on setting up guides and grids.

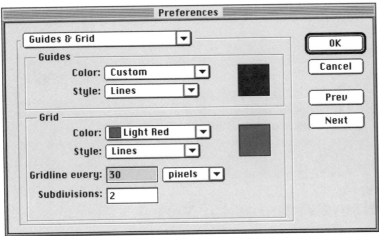

Figure 1-5. *With guides and grids, you can now use Photoshop as a web layout tool*

Creating a browser-safe swatch

To prepare for working on a web graphic, many web designers start by loading a browser-safe color swatch into the Swatches palette. Browser-safe colors are those 216 colors that are compatible between the Macintosh and Windows platforms. These are colors that won't dither when viewed on a 256-color display system. For this reason, many people refer to these colors as "non-dithering" colors. (See Chapters 3 and 4 for more information regarding browser-safe colors.) With the browser-safe swatch, it's easy to paint, draw, or colorize web graphics that look their best on most display systems, as shown in Figure 1-6.

Figure 1-6. *With a browser-safe color swatch at your fingertips, you can readily create images that will look great to the most viewers*

Photoshop 4.0 includes a browser-safe color swatch in the Goodies folder. If you're using an earlier version of Photoshop, you can easily make your own browser-safe swatch, as HotWired's Anna McMillan has done. Here are the steps to making your own browser-safe palette:

1. Open a window containing a simple RGB graphic. It doesn't matter what your window contains, as long as you are in the RGB mode.

2. Choose Image: Mode: Indexed Color to convert to Indexed Color mode.

3. Choose Palette: Custom. Then load a Web palette file. (You can find a Web palette at the Adobe web site: *http://www.adobe.com/ supportservice/custsupport/LIBRARY/2a7a.htm*. Adobe refers to it as a "non-dithering Web palette.")

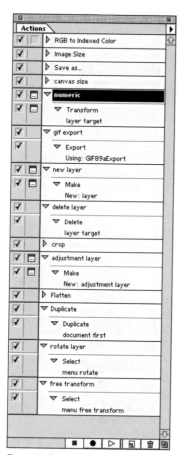

Figure 1-7. *Web designer Steve Jablonsky uses Actions much like a function key, recording even the simplest tasks such as opening the GIF89a Export filter*

4. Choose Mode: Color Table and chose Save, name the file, and place it in a handy folder. Then cancel out of the Color Table dialog.

5. From the Swatches palette, choose Load Swatches or Replace Swatches from the pull-down menu. Select your file in the dialog box and click OK.

6. If you choose Load Swatches, the browser-safe colors are added to the bottom of your existing swatch. If you choose Replace Swatches, the new palette replaces the old colors. These colors will remain in the Swatches palette until the palette is either reset to its default or replaced by another swatch of colors.

Using Actions for web production

The Actions palette is one of the most useful features in Photoshop 4.0. Actions can be used to automate many of the tedious tasks required for producing web graphics. For example, you can automate converting RGB images to Indexed Color mode, resizing batches of images, simulating an animated effect, and applying a consistently used filter. This book highlights several tasks that are best carried out with Actions.

Some web designers use Actions for even the simplest tasks. For example, Figure 1-7 contains a screenshot of Steve Jablonsky's Actions palette, which is always open and accessible when he creates web graphics. Steve has created Actions for such tasks as creating a new layer, adding an adjustment layer, flattening an image, and using the Save As command.

Keep in mind that not everything can be recorded as an Action. For instance, you can't record work done with the various drawing tools or record changes in Preferences or color settings. You can, however, insert a command for these non-recordable acts with the Insert Menu Item command found in the Actions palette.

Calibrating your monitor

Ah, CRT monitor calibration—what a snake pit! Everyone talks about it, but few do it. The reality is that it's quite helpful to have some sort of objective standard in which to view your work. How else will you know how much contrast or brightness to add to your otherwise carefully crafted image or graphic? How will you know when your colors are saturated enough?

Your monitor is your canvas, and you should take a moment to ensure that it is at least in the ballpark when it comes to color and brightness display.

Of course, you don't have to get it perfect. Web designer and long-time new media producer Tom Walker points out that the human visual system is very forgiving. When most people look at a monitor, their expectations are lower than if they look at a printed page. Most display systems are backlit, creating an illusion of quality comparable to a slide. Also, in general, our brain quickly compensates for slight color shifts: for example, it makes an image with an overall bluish cast seem normal.

Photoshop provides a rudimentary method for monitor calibration that relies mostly on subjective visual interpretation, so it's not particularly accurate. If you're really serious about precisely calibrating your monitor, you need to use a color calibration device such as the OpticalCal or Daystar's Colorimeter 24 system, or you'll need to purchase a display system such as Barco or Radius that contains built-in hardware calibration.

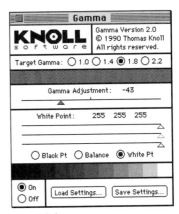

Figure 1-8. *Calibrate your Mac monitor with the Gamma control dialog box*

To calibrate your monitor using only software, follow these steps:

1. Warm up your monitor for at least 30 minutes to give it time to stabilize.

2. Manually adjust the Brightness/Contrast settings on the monitor itself until you are satisfied with the results.

3. Adjust the background color on your computer to a neutral gray. Turn off any desktop patterns. *For Macintosh:* From the Control Panels in the Apple menu, open the Gamma control panel (see Figure 1-8). If Gamma is not there, look in the Goodies folder that came with Photoshop, install the file in your System folder, and restart your machine. *For Windows:* Access the Gamma control dialog box by selecting File: Color Settings: Monitor Setup.

4. Click on White Pt. Hold a piece of true white paper under daylight-like conditions and adjust the three sliders until the monitor white matches the paper. (Sliding the Red pointer will add or subtract red to your monitor, sliding the Green pointer will add or subtract green, and sliding the Blue pointer will add or subtract blue. It takes a little work to get a clean white.)

5. Set your Target Gamma to 1.8. Slide the Gamma Adjustment slider until the patterned gray area at the top of the Gamma window becomes a solid gray.

Gamma-gamma-hey

Gamma for the Mac is actually a global control that affects all programs, while the Windows version method of calibration affects only the monitor display within Photoshop itself.

6. To adjust color balance visually, click on Balance and drag the three slider triangles one at a time until the gray areas in the strip below the slider become a neutral gray.

7. To adjust the black point, click Black Pt and drag the three slider triangles until no color tints appear in the shadow tones in the lower strip and you can see a distinct gradation between each pair of swatches.

8. Save these settings in a folder named "Monitor Settings" inside the Photoshop folder.

Calibrating a monitor for a Windows machine using Photoshop is very similar to calibrating it for a Mac. However, instead of finding the Gamma control panel in the Controls Panels folder, it is accessed by selecting File: Color Settings: Monitor Setup from the Photoshop menu. Once this dialog box is open, follow steps 4–7, typing a target gamma of 1.8 into the window rather than selecting it.

If your monitor has the capability, be sure to regularly degauss it to remove the effects of magnetic pulls that make the images on the monitor look wavy.

Once you've calibrated your monitor, there's still the issue of the gamma differences between Macs and PCs. In general, what looks right on a Macintosh will look dark on a Windows machine. What looks right on a Windows machine will look washed out on a Mac. The culprit is gamma.

Gamma is the mathematical measurement used to describe a monitor's contrast and brightness. Gamma can be corrected or adjusted in several ways: in the image, in the operating system, and on the monitor itself. When you use GIF and JPEG image formats, there is no way for the end user system to determine if you've applied any gamma correction to the image, and if so, what value was used. Some file formats such as TIFF and PNG contain gamma source declarations that automatically compensate for any variations between display systems.

There are a couple of things you can do to minimize this problem. Assuming that your monitor has been calibrated:

*   When you create an image on a Mac system, make the image at least 20% brighter.

*   When you create an image on a PC system, make the image at least 20% darker.

*   Include a grayscale target on your site so users can calibrate their systems to match yours.

- Use the PNG file format, which automatically adjusts gamma to match different display systems (see Appendix A, *The PNG Format*).

Take the time

It pays to take a few moments to set your preferences, load a set of browser-safe colors, and calibrate your monitor. Not only will you benefit in terms of smaller file size, but you'll also focus on web-specific issues that will put you in the state of mind to produce images and graphics that look great and download quickly.

CHAPTER TWO

IMPROVING PHOTOS FOR THE WEB

Photographs destined for the Web can benefit from Photoshop's powerful image processing capabilities: contrast control, color optimizing, image sharpening, and elimination of dust, scratches, and electronic noise. When Photoshop's tools are applied properly, the best qualities of an existing image are enhanced.

What happens if a photograph is not properly prepared and processed? Just look at Figure 2-1, a Web Review article on the 1997 World Wide Web Conference. Some of the photos look washed out. In others you can't see the faces because they are too dark. In short, because these photos weren't properly prepared before they were put on the Web, they decrease the effectiveness of the entire page.

This chapter shows you how to use Photoshop to fix many of the problems illustrated by this example and more. You'll also learn a couple of tricks to optimize images taken from digital cameras. (Preparing images or graphics for a particular file format is the subject of later chapters.) Figure 2-2 shows a makeover of the Web Review page using techniques discussed in this chapter. Much better, no?

Let's go through the various corrections I made to these images:

- In the first photo, the colors are washed out. The background is full of electronic "noise" and there is a glare in the glasses caused by the digital camera's flash.

  To fix it, I adjusted the curves (Image: Adjust: Curves) by clicking on the Auto button. I used the Clone tool to spot the glasses to reduce the glare. Then I applied an Unsharp Mask (Filter: Sharpen: Unsharp Mask) set at a radius of .4 pixels and 100%. Then I applied the Dust and Scratches (Filter: Noise: Dust &

In this chapter

- Every photo requires individual attention
- Removing dust and other artifacts
- Sharpening a blurred photo
- Getting rid of red-eye
- Adjusting contrast and increasing dynamic range
- Getting the color right
- Resizing
- Cropping your images
- Getting better video grabs
- Improving digital camera photos
- Moving ahead

Figure 2-1. *In this example, improperly prepared photos detract, rather than enhance, a web page*

Scratches) filter with a 1-pixel radius to the selected background. I applied a Gaussian blur (Filter: Blur: Gaussian Blur) with a 5-pixel radius to the blue channel. And finally I applied an Unsharp Mask with a .3-pixel radius to the entire image.

Figure 2-2. *In this makeover, the photos have been processed to compensate for flatness, color cast, and overexposure*

- In the second photo, the foreground is too light. The people in the background are out of focus.

  Again, I applied auto curves and an Unsharp Mask, this time with an amount of 150% and a radius of 1.1. The picture still

---

Work from copies

Whenever possible, work off a copy of your original high-resolution file and keep your original for other purposes, such as creating new images at different resolutions.

---

appears slightly out of focus. Not much I could do about that. I used the Burn tool set at 50% and Midtones to selectively burn in the highlights.

- In the third photo, the person in the foreground is too dark.

  I applied an Unsharp Mask (100%, .6 radius) to the entire image. Then I selected the text areas and applied another Unsharp Mask at the same settings. I tried to use auto curves but it didn't help much. Instead, I selectively applied the Dodge tool to the face to open up the shadows.

- In the fourth photo, the colors are flat and the person in the foreground is too light.

  I selectively burned in the foreground person. I increased the overall saturation of the image by 14% (Image: Adjust: Hue/Saturation). Then, using the Sponge tool, I selectively added saturation to the faces.

Although the procedures discussed in this chapter can be applied as well to illustrations or other digitized art, we have purposefully chosen photography as our main focus. This is because viewers are less forgiving when there is something technically wrong with a photograph. For the most part, they know what a photo should look like and, if their expectations are not met—for example, if a supposedly realistic portrait looks green—they'll probably question the quality of the page and your skills and ability as a web designer.

Every photo requires individual attention

There is no such thing as a typical web photograph. The content of each photo varies, and photos come from a variety of sources, such as digital cameras, video frame grabs, and scans from prints or slides. Each source can technically affect the way a photo looks.

Because every photo is different, each one requires individual attention before it is placed on the Web. It's helpful to think of this activity as an art in itself rather than just a technical procedure. With the help of Photoshop you can intelligently peel away the grime and dirt to reveal the masterpiece beneath. (OK, there's not always a masterpiece beneath, but you can almost always improve a photo with the techniques described here.)

Of course there are times when a batch of photographs shares a common problem—for example, a similar colorcast caused by a poor scan. In situations like this, you can create a Photoshop action from the Actions palette to automate the process of correcting the problem.

Evaluating the photo

After you open a file in Photoshop, the first thing you should do is identify problems associated with the specific photograph. You can readily handle these problems:

- Dust, scratches, or other artifacts that are left over from the digitizing process.

- Lack of contrast (or dynamic range) that makes a photograph look dull or flat, or, conversely, too much contrast that blows out vital details.

- Ugly color casts caused by processing and ambient lighting conditions—for example, a sick green cast resulting from taking a picture under fluorescent lights.

- Wasted space that adds kilobytes, but no needed detail, to the final outcome.

- "Red-eye" caused by camera flash bouncing back from the retina of a person or animal.

- Out-of-focus or blurred images.

Depending on how flawed your photograph is, the process of fixing it can be time consuming. Allow yourself the time to do the job right, but take into account that the Web can be forgiving. At 72 dpi, scratches and dust aren't as noticeable, and because every monitor is different, precise color work is rarely appreciated.

Giving images the eagle eye

At Second Story, Brad Johnson is keenly aware that each photograph requires individual attention. His company has created web sites for such photograph-centric institutions and companies as the National Geographic Society and Kyocera (makers of Yashica and Contact cameras). Figure C-1 (see color pages) shows the impact of photography on a National Geographic page designed by Second Story.

Brad and his partner Julie Beeler have worked with every imaginable type of photographic image, ranging from corporate product shots to action-filled snaps of white-water rafting. The images are digitized and sent to him on Kodak Photo CDs or Zip disks.

His evaluation of each photo actually begins before he looks at it on his monitor. At the onset, he inquires about any special rules or restrictions placed on a particular image. For example, some National Geographic and stock agency photographs cannot be cropped or altered in any way except for minor color correction and resizing.

Keep it authentic

Many historical photos and other images have scratches. If you want to keep the authentic historical look and feel, don't apply the techniques for removing dust and scratches.

Initially, he looks at the image for any of the problems listed above. The digital files he gets from National Geographic have already been cleaned up and are nearly flawless—there are no scratches or electronic noise to speak of, and the colors are correct—but files from other sources often need work. Photographs from digital cameras, he's learned, will almost always be flat and need increased color saturation. He doesn't make any generalizations about Photo CD images since they all vary depending on how they were scanned and who did the scanning.

After he determines what needs to be done, Brad jumps in and starts to work. For him there is no particular order to follow. However, he always waits to resize images until the end because this action throws away data that can't be retrieved.

Removing dust and other artifacts

It's a rare digital photo that doesn't contain either dust marks or a stray pixel or two caused by electronic "noise." If these flaws are present in your digital file, they will be quite apparent when you open up your photograph. There are several different ways to rid your photo of these distractions with Photoshop.

Using the noise filters

Under the Filters: Noise menu there are three filters useful for eliminating flaws that are sprinkled throughout a large region of your photograph:

- *Despeckle* diminishes noise by subtly blurring an image. However, some detail is preserved because this filter blurs everything except the edges in an image, where significant shifts in color occur.

- The *Median* filter blends the brightness of pixels and discards pixels that are radically different from adjacent pixels. Adjust the Radius slider to determine how much variation in brightness values the filter looks for. A value that is too high causes a blurred image.

- The *Dust & Scratches* filter gives you the most control of these filters. Use the Radius and Threshold sliders in this option to set the removal size of dust or scratches.

You can quickly see that in order to get good results with any of these filters, your photo invariably blurs (see "Sharpening a blurred photo" later in this chapter). For this reason, it is best to apply filters only on regions of your photograph lacking important detail, such as the background. Fix the flaws that exist in areas of important detail with the Rubber Stamp tool (found in the Toolbox), which duplicates the pixels surrounding an offensive scratch or unwanted mark and "clones" over it.

(The Smudge and Blur tools, also found in the Toolbox, usually are not good alternatives to the Rubber Stamp tool because they smear and blend pixels and create an unrealistic effect.)

Lines of distinction

There are times when the lines of distinction between image processing and image creation blur. Take, for example, the work of Brad Johnson shown in Figure C-2 in the color insert. What looks like an ancient, time-weary photograph is actually created mostly in Photoshop. Brad used a photograph he took of the Mexican site of Chichen Itza and then applied many of the image-processing techniques described in this chapter to produce a stunning effect. By looking at each layer, shown in Figure 2-3, you can see exactly what he did:

- *Layer 0* is the original photograph that Brad took at Chichen Itza in Mexico.

- The next layer up is a copy of *Layer 0* with a Gaussian blur applied to despeckle the original image. Opacity is set at 58% and the blending mode is Normal.

- The *antique 1* layer is a scanned painting that Brad added for effect. Opacity is set at 23% and the blending mode is Soft Light.

- The next layer contains some faint lines or "scratches" that give the photograph an aged look. Opacity is set at 21% and the blending mode is Soft Light.

- The next layer contains a black border.

- The final layer contains a light orange "glaze" (Red = 255, Green = 204, Blue = 102). Opacity is 58% and the blending mode is Color Burn.

If you try to duplicate this effect, be sure that you work with an appropriate photograph, one that lends itself to this "turn-of-the-century" look.

Cleaning up photos with Gaussian blur

Brad Johnson generally avoids using any of the filters mentioned previously to clean up his images since he doesn't like the way they blur his pictures. Most of the time he uses the Rubber Stamp tool, but when the noise is widespread throughout a photo, he's discovered a method using layers that he much prefers.

Brad cleans up his photos by following these steps:

1. He creates a duplicate of the layer containing his photograph or image that he wants to work on (Layer: Duplicate Layer).

Figure 2-3. *Layers palette for the Chichen Itza image*

Figure 2-4. *Moiré patterns result when printed images are scanned*

Figure 2-5. *Moiré patterns were removed by scanning this printed photograph at twice the needed resolution*

2. He applies a Gaussian blur to the new layer (Filter: Blur: Gaussian Blur), setting the radius to 2.0 or less, but sometimes higher, depending on the effect he wants.

3. He leaves his blending mode on Normal, but adjusts the opacity between 30–70%.

4. Finally, he merges the two layers.

Brad applied this method—and other useful methods described elsewhere in this chapter—in the *scratches* layer of his Chichen Itza image (Figures C-2 and 2-3), as described in the "Lines of distinction" sidebar.

Eliminating moiré patterns

Moiré patterns result when you try to scan a picture containing halftone dots, from a newspaper, magazine, or book, as shown in Figure 2-4. Steve Jablonsky of Imaginary Studios has found that by scanning the pictures at twice the resolution he needs, then resizing them in Photoshop, the moiré pattern virtually disappears, as in Figure 2-5.

Sharpening a blurred photo

A blurred photo can be a result of many things, such as camera or subject movement, improper focus, imprecise scanning, or too radical resampling. With Photoshop you can sharpen a blurred photo to a degree; however, there is no substitute for a properly shot or scanned photograph.

Photoshop's filters and tools for sharpening include:

• The *Sharpen* filters (Filter: Sharpen or Filter: Sharpen More). These filters globally increase the contrast of adjacent pixels, with Sharpen More being equivalent to applying Sharpen several times. You can control the amount of sharpening by repeatedly applying these filters.

• The *Sharpen Edges* filter (Filter: Sharpen: Sharpen Edges). This filter sharpens only the areas of major brightness change and leaves smooth areas untouched.

• The *Sharpen* tool found in the Toolbox (toggles with Blur), which sharpens soft edges in an image.

• The *Unsharp Mask* filter (Filter: Sharpen: Unsharp Mask), which creates a blurred negative version of the image and averages this copy with the original. You can control the percentage of sharpening, the number of pixels surrounding the edge pixels affected by the sharpening (radius), and how much brightness difference exists between two pixels before they are considered edge pixels (threshold).

Undoubtedly, Unsharp Mask is the mostly widely used sharpening filter by web producers. Through your customized settings, Unsharp Mask selectively applies sharpening only to the areas that you specify.

How do you know which settings to use? It depends on both the resolution and type of image you are working with. You'll have to experiment on your own, but assuming that your image is destined for the Web and is therefore 72 dpi and no larger than 640 × 480 pixels, here are some suggestions:

- For images that contain lots of detail (such as architectural photos), try setting your percentage at 150% and your radius at 2. (I always leave threshold settings at zero.)

- For images that contain expanses of similar color and tone (such as a portrait), try setting your percentage to 100% with a radius of 1 pixel.

Keep in mind that the higher the resolution, the less pronounced the effect of the Unsharp Mask and the higher the settings you need to apply.

Getting rid of red-eye

Red-eye is caused when a strong source of light, usually a strobe flash, is aimed directly at a dilated pupil. It's a common occurrence when a picture is taken with a flash in a dark room because that is when the eye's pupil is at its widest and the light reflects back from the pupil itself, giving that all too familiar demonic look. It's easy to fix it in Photoshop:

- Use the Sponge tool to desaturate the red (click and hold the Dodge or Burn tool to access the Sponge tool).

- Select the red area using the Lasso selection tool and replace the red with another color drawn from the surrounding area with the Eyedropper + tool. You can also desaturate the selected area by choosing Image: Adjust: Saturation and moving the saturation slider far to the left.

Whatever method you use, it's best to magnify the area containing the red-eye to its maximum before you start.

Adjusting contrast and increasing dynamic range

A low-contrast photograph is like a meal without spice—the picture (food) might be good, but without contrast (spice) it's dull. A high-

---

Scan out of focus

Another way of ridding a photograph or other scanned art of the moiré pattern is to alter the position of the printed photograph on the scanner and, if your scanner allows, scan slightly out of focus. It also helps to apply the Despeckle filter (Filters: Noise: Despeckle) afterwards in Photoshop.

contrast photograph is, well, too spicy. The true flavor and content are lost. For the most part, you can determine whether a photograph has contrast problems simply by looking at your photograph on the monitor. The photo in Figure C-3 of a Japanese Shinto priest taken at sunset clearly has too much contrast. The photo in Figure C-4 has a good dynamic range.

If you're more comfortable getting a precise mathematical rather than visual interpretation of your photograph, you should use Photoshop's histogram (Image: Histogram). The histogram graphically represents tonal distribution in an image. High-contrast images show up as two peaks on the graph at either end of the brightness area. Low-contrast images show up as a mound in only one region of the graph.

If measurements show pixels falling between a small portion of gray values and none in other areas, there is a small dynamic range present, which for the most part is undesirable, and you'll need to apply the following corrections. A wide distribution shows a large dynamic range, which for the most part is desirable (see Figure C-4).

Once you have determined that your photo's contrast needs adjustment, you can select one of Photoshop's several tonal control commands found under Image: Adjust. For our purposes, the more useful tools are Curves, Levels, and Brightness/Contrast:

- *Levels* allows you to set the highlight, midtone, and shadow values.

- *Curves* provides a visual graph that allows you to adjust not only the highlight, midtone, and shadow values, but also any value at any point on the graph.

- *Brightness/Contrast* provides a slider that affects the relationships between pixels: for example, making an adjacent pixel brighter while making another darker. The Brightness slider affects all the pixels equally.

Most web producers work with either Levels or Curves. Although Brightness/Contrast is the easiest to use, it offers only limited control over the image.

As you experiment with these tools, watch as they apply their changes to the image on the screen in real time. Don't think only in terms of keeping detail in the shadow and highlight areas; consider the overall look and feel of the image. Sometimes a high-contrast image where the highlights are burned out works. Also keep in mind that Photoshop can improve a poorly exposed or scanned image only up to a point, which is why the original quality of the image and scan are so important.

Tinting to make the photo pop

Brad Johnson immediately saw particular problems with the photograph shown in Figure 2-6. The silvery surface of the camera looked flat when viewed on a monitor. Increasing the contrast didn't help because the smooth look of metal disappeared. To correct the problem, Brad pulled a trick out of his large hat—he actually tinted the photograph. The tint isn't noticeable, but it gave the silver the pop that he wanted. This is how he did it:

Figure 2-6. *The original photo was flat and dull*

1. He created a new layer, called *color burn,* where he placed a copy of the selected camera.

2. He filled this selection with a bright violet color (Red = 153, Green = 51, Blue = 255). He set the blending mode for this layer to color burn and set the opacity at 5%. Figure 2-7 shows the effect of the tinting.

3. He then created an Adjustment Layer above the original photograph (from the Layers palette, select New Adjustment Layer), using Levels to set the tone and contrast.

4. He added a drop-shadow and a white background. The web page with this final image is shown in Figure 2-8.

Figure 2-7. *After adding a violet tint and a Levels adjustment, the camera pops from the page*

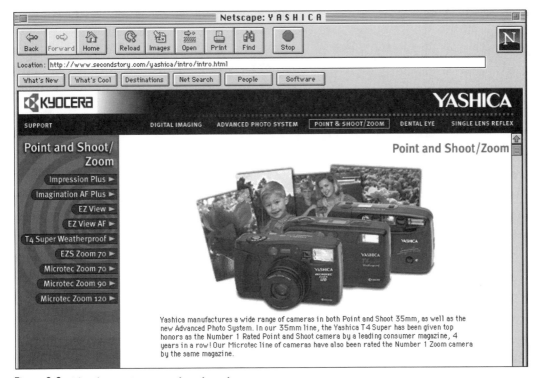

Figure 2-8. *The photo as it appeared on the web page*

Figure 2-9. *In the original photograph the legs are too dark*

Figure 2-10. *Steve Jablonsky created a mask of the detective photo that allowed only the best parts of each image to show through*

Getting realistic results with Photo CD and masks

The following method, provided by Steve Jablonsky of Imaginary Studios, is a great way to increase the dynamic tonal range of your image. However, this method is not for everyone. You must use Eastman Kodak's Photo CD process to digitize and store your images. If you aren't using this process, you might consider doing so after you read this section.

Steve knew he could use any number of ways in Photoshop to improve a photograph he took of two detectives that he wanted to include in "Homicide: Second Shift," an online series that compliments the popular television program, *Homicide*. As shown in Figure 2-9, the detectives' legs were nearly invisible because their trousers blended into the dark background.

He could have worked on the problem with the Curves or Levels tools, for example. But, since the original photo was shot on normal film and transferred to Kodak's Photo CD, Steve realized he could use a better way—one that gave him more precise control over the final outcome.

When a photo is digitized and saved on a Photo CD, it can be opened in a variety of resolutions. It can also be opened using different gamma settings, each of which gives a different result. For example, if a photo is opened using a gamma of 1.4 and then opened a second time using a gamma of 1.8, the shadows in the second version will be less pronounced.

You can achieve more realistic results with gamma because it is a non-linear way of applying tonal and color correction. (In order to acquire an image from Photo CD in this way, you'll need to download the Photo CD Acquire module from Kodak's web site, *www.kodak.com*. It's free. Be sure to download Version 2.2, because, older versions don't allow you to specify gamma.)

This is what Steve did to give his detectives the legs they needed:

1. He opened one file at a gamma of 1.4 at 512 × 768 pixels, as shown in Figure 2-9. At this setting the legs were too dark, but the rest of the picture was fine.

2. Then he opened a second version at a gamma of 1.8, where the pants were perfect, but the upper bodies were too light.

3. He cut and pasted this version onto a layer above the first version.

4. Then he masked out areas of the 1.8 gamma version that he didn't want, including most of the upper parts of the body, as shown in Figure 2-10.

5. When he combined the two layers he got exactly what he wanted.

For the final image, shown in Figure 2-11, he cut and pasted the detectives onto a realistic looking set.

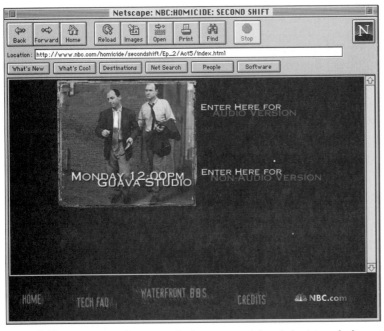

Figure 2-11. *The results of Steve's work: the pants, and the whole picture, look great*

Getting the color right

Color casts can be a result of poor scanning, or they may be inherent in the original image. In either case, it's an issue if you fall short of a realistic look. (Potatoes, for example, are not very appetizing when they are presented with a sick greenish cast—an effect that can be caused by shooting color film under fluorescent lighting).

Photoshop's color tools

Photoshop provides several commands—both automatic and manual—for removing colors, and increasing or decreasing color saturation. These commands are all found under Image: Adjust.

Try it with Adjustments

Photoshop 4.0 includes adjustment layers, one of the most important Photoshop features to date. In the Layers palette, select New Adjustment Layer from the pull-down menu. This option allows you to apply color and tonal corrections to a specific layer, and then, if you decide later not to use the correction, to discard the adjustment layer with no change whatsoever to the original layer. (In other versions of Photoshop, when you apply a tonal or color correction you are stuck with the changes unless you Undo immediately.)

Don't forget your borders!

If your image contains a black border, be sure to either remove this border or work only on a selection within the black border. The border fools Photoshop's auto correction tools into thinking the image is darker than it actually is.

The quickest auto correction is Auto Levels, but you can also auto-correct with Levels or Curves. Auto-correction not only attempts to create pure white and pure black and adjust the color range, but also attempts to balance the color cast by adjusting the RGB components of the image. Remember that by using selection tools you always have the option of applying color changes to specific areas of the image or to the entire image.

Manual correction can be applied using the tools under Image: Adjust. For quick, global color correction, use the Levels and Curves commands. With Levels, you simply adjust the sliders until you get the results you want. Using Curves is more awkward because you don't work linearly. The best way to use Curves is to find the midpoint of the curve, click, and then rotate the point in a circle until you get the color correction you want.

To remove unwanted colors, use Color Balance, which adjusts the balance of colors in the image. Hue/Saturation makes global or selective color changes to the color tint (hue), purity of color (saturation) or the lightness of the color. Replace Color and Selective Color allow for even more selective and precise color correction.

Keep in mind that a color image is made up of red, green, and blue layers of color. With Levels and Curves, you can select and control any of one these colors, affecting the entire image.

Variations is another handy option, although it isn't as precise as the other methods described in this section. With it, you can visually adjust an image's color balance, contrast, and saturation. As you click on small color-correct previews, the original image changes accordingly. Optional sample corrections are also included.

Finally, you might consider that color correction can be likened to a black hole—you go in but don't seem to come out. It's so easy to overdo color corrections, especially when you consider that color is subjective and everyone perceives colors a bit differently. Remember, on the Web, your results will vary from monitor to monitor anyway, so don't spend too much time on this step. Fix the obvious problems and then move on.

Removing a blue tint with Variations and Levels

When Discovery's Brian Frick received a digital file containing several photos from the Dominican Republic, he was told that the person using the digital camera forgot to set the white balance. All the frames contained a blue tint. Brian rid the photo of the annoying color cast by using Variations (see Figure C-5) to pick the image with the least amount of blue tint. Then he applied Photoshop's Levels and improved the photo even more. He gave the colors a final tweak with Hue/Saturation. Figure C-6 shows the final image on the web site.

Resizing

Resizing or resampling images is a common task for web producers, and deceptively simple.

To resize an image in Photoshop, follow these steps:

1. Select Image: Image Size.
2. Enter the desired dimensions under Pixel Dimensions.

Unless you want to distort your image, be sure that Constrain Proportions is checked. For the best results, keep the interpolation method set at Bicubic, the default setting. (In Photoshop 4.0, you can set the sampling method in the Image Size dialog. In other versions, set the sampling method in Preferences.)

It is tempting to just enter the desired values and leave it at that. However, if you start with a 640 × 480 pixel file and resize directly to, say, 100 × 100 pixels, you are making a huge mistake. You will likely create a smaller image that looks "soft" or mushy, that no amount of sharpening will help. Instead, reduce your file size no more than 50% at a time and apply the Unsharp Mask slightly after each step.

Your Unsharp Mask settings will depend on the quality of the image you are working with, but for the resolution of this example I suggest you start at 75%, with a .4 pixel radius and 0 threshold, then continue to reduce the percentage and radius as you resample. Also adjust your Unsharp Mask settings for each resolution, starting at a higher setting for the larger file and then reducing the numbers as the file gets smaller.

For a 640 × 480 pixel file, you would start by resampling to 320 × 240 pixels, then going to 160 × 120 pixels, then to 100 × 100 pixels, applying Unsharp Mask after each step. If you have a batch of similarly sized images that need to be resized, you can create a Photoshop 4.0 Action to resize in increments.

Cropping your images

The most simple and effective way to reduce an image file size (short of resizing) is to crop the image down to its most important parts. Figure 2-12 shows an image before and after cropping. The cropped image is 20K smaller than the original.

Be consistent

If you are processing a batch of photos that are destined to be shown together on the same web page or site, be consistent. Stay in the same ballpark with contrast, tone, and saturation.

Figure 2-12. *Cropping away the unnecessary areas created a file more than 30 percent smaller*

The actual work of cropping a photograph (or any other web graphic) is easy with Photoshop's Crop tool, found in the Toolbox. In Photoshop 4.0, you'll find it on the pull-out menu from the Marquee in the upper-left corner. Select the area that you want to save, then crop. You can also specify the size and resolution of the cropped area with the Crop tool's options by double-clicking on its icon in the Toolbox.

Another way to crop is to use the Crop command. This command, found under Image, discards areas outside of a rectangular selection and keeps the original resolution of the image intact. Just select the area you want to retain with the Marquee and then Image: Crop.

Once the Crop tool or Crop command is applied, areas outside of the selection will be cut. The result is a smaller image, and a smaller file size. Cropping irretrievably throws away data unless you immediately Undo, so be sure of your decision or save a backup copy of your uncropped original.

Getting better video grabs

Moving video, such as a VHS tape and broadcast television, contains up to 30 frames (or 60 interlaced fields) of still images per second, with each frame containing about 640 × 480 pixels at 24 bits of image information. Any one of these frames can be "grabbed" directly from a VCR, a television broadcast, or a camcorder by the use of special equipment.

The actual quality of this still image varies, depending on the quality of the videotape, the quality of the broadcast, and the quality of the equipment you use to grab the frame. With a little help from Photoshop's image-processing capabilities described in this chapter, the frame is usually suitable for the Web.

SF Gate's webmaster Steve Kruschwiz recommends grabbing video frames at twice the resolution of the final size that they will appear on the Web. He does this regularly with frames he grabs from the San Francisco travel show *Bay Area Backroads*, as shown in Figure 2-13.

Time lags with grabs

Grabbing a frame from a video is like shooting a camera with a sticky trigger. There is a lag between the time you "click" the shutter and the moment the frame is grabbed. Luckily, if you don't get the frame you want, you can just rewind and start over. Nothing is lost except your time.

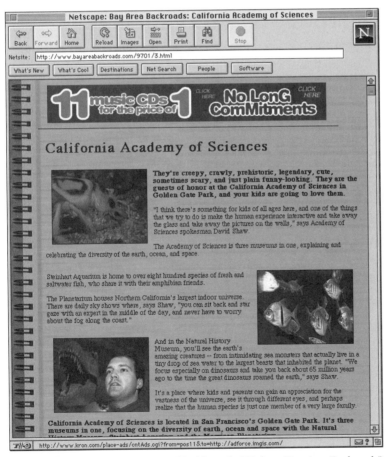

Figure 2-13. *These "photos" were grabbed from the TV show "Bay Area Backroads"*

Steve uses a Super VHS deck and an Apple video player card to grab the frames he wants. Although he ends up using about a dozen images for the site, he starts out by grabbing about 30. Since the images run at 160 × 120 pixels, he sets his player to grab a frame at 320 × 240 pixels. After he has grabbed the frames he wants, he adjusts the color and contrast visually using Photoshop's Levels (Image: Adjust). Depending on how much time he has, he goes in and plays with the Hue: Saturation controls as well. Occasionally, when he has time, he uses the Burn and Dodge tools. Steve admits that he feels there is always more he can do to improve a particular image, but he's usually constrained by time.

When he's finished, he applies the Unsharp Mask (Filter: Sharpen). Then he uses the Crop tool to reduce the image to 160 × 120 pixels. Finally, he applies Unsharp Mask a second time.

Improving digital camera photos

Digital cameras and the Web are a match made in heaven. With digital cameras, you don't need film, chemical processing, or time-consuming conversions from analog to digital formats. Photos produced by these cameras can be instantly put on a web page from anywhere in the world—a riverboat in the Grand Canyon or the most desolate corner of Siberia. Best of all, because the destination of the image is a relatively low-resolution electronic screen, almost any of the plethora of digital cameras—including the inexpensive ones—will meet your needs. However, because of the way that digital cameras capture data, they often need help from Photoshop.

Making skin tones look better

Most digital cameras rely on electronic sensors called *charge coupled devices* (CCDs) to capture color information. In general, CCDs do a good job of capturing red and green colors, but have more trouble capturing blue. The more expensive digital cameras are equipped with better sensors and more sophisticated electronics and do a better (but still not perfect) job with blue.

You can see the problem by looking at Figure 2-14 and 2-15. The photo was taken with a consumer-level digital camera. Figure 2-14 shows the blue channel. Notice how blotchy the image appears. These blotches will also be evident in the final RGB composite, degrading the overall effect of the image. If you look at Figure 2-15, you'll see the green channel isolated. The green channel looks much smoother due to the sensor's ability to capture this color better.

Figure 2-14. *The weak blue channel degrades the entire image*

To compensate for the degradation caused by poor blue capture,
follow these steps:

1. From the Channels palette, isolate the blue channel by clicking
   the Eye icons for the other colors.

2. Select Filter: Blur: Gaussian Blur. Apply as much of this filter as
   necessary to diminish the chunky look. Don't worry if it seems
   like you are over-blurring the image. The other channels are not

Figure 2-15. *The green channel captures the image well*

affected and the blurring in the blue channel will not be noticeable in the final image.

3. To view the composite effects, from the Channels palette, click the far-left box at the RGB level to turn on all the Eye icons. Notice that the chunky effect caused by the poorly sampled blue channel is gone, as shown in Figure 2-15.

This method is especially effective on skin tones where the adjustments are most noticeable, but it can also be used to improve just about any image taken with a digital camera.

You can have similarly improved results when you apply this technique to images that have been scanned on low-cost scanners, which also rely on CCDs.

Warming up with tints

Brad Johnson of Second Story has found that the images produced on digital cameras are invariably a bit cold for his taste. Borrowing a technique that he learned from his life as a painter, he applies a glaze or tint to warm up an image. His technique for doing this is similar to the one that he applied to the silver camera, described earlier in this chapter. Instead of applying a bright violet color, he applies a yellow-orange. To warm up an image, he follows these steps:

1. First he creates a new layer above the layer containing the digital camera image: from the Layers palette he selects New Layer.

2. He fills this layer with yellow-orange (Red = 255, Green = 102, Blue = 0).

3. He selects Color Burn from the blending modes. Then he plays with the opacity until he gets it right.

Brad also uses his Gaussian blur technique to clean up shots taken with a digital camera and make them look less electronic. He creates a duplicate layer containing his photograph, applies a Gaussian blur to the duplicate layer, leaves the blending mode at Normal, and adjusts the opacity. When he is finished, he merges the two layers.

Figure C-7 shows a photograph to which Brad applied both of these techniques.

Moving ahead

Once you've finished cleaning, correcting, and cropping your web photo, you still have ahead of you the tasks of choosing a file format and otherwise preparing your image for the Web. If you've followed the suggestions outlined in this chapter, you are well on your way to creating a web photo that will embellish, not detract from the rest of your work.

CHAPTER THREE

MAKING GREAT GIFs

W hat's more important—a site that loads fast or a site that looks great? If you simply convert your art to a GIF or JPEG file, accept the default settings, and save the file, chances are you'll wind up with graphics that are neither good enough nor small enough.

Through the next four chapters, you'll learn tons of tricks and techniques to make the most effective web graphics with Photoshop. In this chapter, we'll deal with converting existing images to GIF. Chapter 4, *Creating GIFs from Scratch*, covers creating GIF files from scratch. Chapter 5, *Special Effects with Transparent GIFs*, covers transparent GIFs. And Chapter 6, *JPEG: All the Color You Want*, shows you how to make the best JPEG files.

GIF or JPEG?

The primary decision you have to make for any web graphic is file format. Make the wrong choice and you'll wind up with files that are larger than they need to be and images that don't look as good as they could. Make the right choice and you'll be assured that your images load fast, look reasonably good, and work for users of all platforms and screen displays.

Although there are many graphic file formats, GIF and JPEG are the most important ones that you have to know about for work on the Web, since they are directly supported by web browsers. All versions of Photoshop will read and write the basic GIF and JPEG formats. Photoshop 4.0 (and earlier versions of Photoshop, with the help of plug-ins) will read and write later variations of the formats (such as progressive rendering for JPEGs and transparency for GIFs). Photoshop 4.0 also offers limited support for PNG, a new file format that is gaining widespread support (and which is discussed in more detail in Appendix A, *The PNG Format*).

Both the GIF and JPEG formats give you ways to control the file size of your web graphics, a critical feature considering the Web's current limited bandwidth capabilities. JPEG does this by compressing and actually throwing away data it considers unnecessary. GIF controls file size through a combination of compression and color reduction through a process called indexing, which is discussed in the next section.

So, GIF or JPEG? The answer depends on the image's content and on how you want it to appear on your web page.

There are a number of crucial differences between the two formats:

- GIF is an 8-bit format. JPEG is a 24-bit format.

- GIF uses lossless compression. JPEG uses lossy compression.

- GIF uses a color index. JPEG uses the full range of 16 million colors.

- GIF supports transparency. JPEG does not.

In general, GIF works better for images with flat colors and JPEG works better with photographic images, but there are many exceptions to the rule. Table 3-1 gives some general rules for when and when not to use GIF and JPEG.

Table 3-1. *When to use and avoid GIF and JPEG*

	Use for:	Avoid with:
GIF	Graphics containing limited numbers of colors, or intricate detail that you want to maintain.	Large photographic images or illustrations that contain a lot of color, unless you want to create a floating effect.
	Floating graphics from the page.	
	Creating a simple animation (with the latest GIF file format).	
	Browser-safe colors—colors that won't dither or change when viewed on an 8-bit monitor.	
JPEG	Most photographic images and continuous-tone art that contain subtle shifts in color.	Text or graphics that contain detailed edges.

Those are the rules of thumb. In the real world, things are a little less cut and dried. Take a look at Figures C-8 to C-13 in the color insert to see some actual situations and the decisions that web designers made.

Indexing your image

The most important thing to know about GIF files is that they're *indexed* images. That is, the file contains an index, or a palette, of all the colors in the image. Because GIF is an 8-bit format, the maximum number of colors in a GIF file is 256. This palette is used to assign a color to each pixel in the image. Actually, each pixel is assigned an index number and color values are associated with the index number. For instance, index number 22 may be given a navy blue color, and number 23 may be given sky blue, etc. In the GIF file format, one index number can be tagged as transparent. We'll discuss GIF transparency in Chapter 5.

Figures C-14 and C-15 make the point. Figure C-14 shows a simple illustration created by the artist James Yang and its color index. You can clearly see how the colors in the index are displayed in the image. In Figure C-15, we have the exact same image, but a different color index. The image changes accordingly.

When you realize how the index affects the image, you can see what havoc would be created if you applied the wrong index to an image.

Here are the basic steps for converting a standard RGB image (Photoshop format, TIFF, JPEG, etc.) to GIF:

1. Convert your RGB image to Indexed Color mode (Image: Mode: Indexed Color).

2. In the Indexed Color dialog box, select your palette, bit depth, and dithering preferences.

3. Save (or export) the file as a GIF.

Let's take a look at Photoshop's Indexed Color dialog box, shown in Figure 3-1. This dialog box includes options for palette, color depth, and dithering.

Palette options

The options under Palette are Exact, System, Web, Uniform and Adaptive. As a web artist, you are concerned only with Web, Adaptive, and Exact.

- *Adaptive palette* is Photoshop's interpretation of the best possible color palette for your image. As you look at images in Photoshop, this option will almost always look the best. For photographic images, this is the option that works the best on the Web. For images with flat colors, however, it's another story.

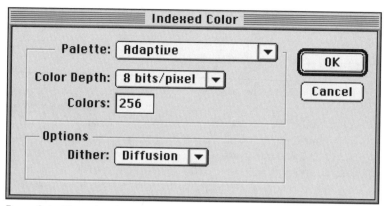

Figure 3-1. *The Indexed Color dialog box*

- *Web palette* is the 216-color palette that Netscape, Internet Explorer, and all other web browsers use. Using this palette on images with large amounts of flat colors will eliminate dithering. Use it on a photograph and you won't be happy.

- *Exact palette* is simply the exact colors found in the image. If your image has more than 256 colors, this option is unavailable. While Exact palette has its uses, as we'll see later, *Adaptive* and *Web* are far more useful.

Color depth options

The next option is *color depth*. Bit depth defines the number of colors in the image. Table 3-2 shows how many colors you get at each bit setting. When converting a full-color image, Photoshop will often set this value at 8 bits, or 256 colors. In the interest of reducing file size, you may want to reduce the color depth. Try setting your image to 7 bits. If it looks great, try it at 6 bits. Choose the fewest amount of colors at which your image is acceptable.

Table 3-2. *Bit depth and number of colors*

Bits:	Creates this size color palette:
8	256
7	128
6	64
5	32
4	16
3	8
2	4

Dithering options

The final option is *dithering*, a process that rearranges pixels to simulate colors that aren't actually in the color palette by combining
available colors into patterns that approximate the missing colors. If
you choose dithering, you should always use *diffusion* dithering. In
general, you should dither continuous-tone images, but not images
with flat colors. We'll talk more about the distinction between these
kinds of images in the next section.

Using the Adaptive palette

If you are just looking for a quick and easy way to prepare your
images or graphics for the GIF format, you can use either of these
methods:

- If you have a continuous-tone image with more than 256 colors
  (such as a photograph, a colorful illustration, or anti-aliased
  text), use the Adaptive palette set at 8 bits (256 colors) with diffusion dither.

- If your graphic contains less than 256 colors, use the Exact palette with no dither.

When you choose the Adaptive palette, Photoshop creates a palette
of most commonly used colors in the image. In most cases, your original will have more than 256 colors, so the Adaptive palette will use
every available color (256). If your image has less than 256 colors,
Photoshop will default to the Exact palette and use only the number
of colors present. That is, if your original had 83 colors, your GIF's
color palette will contain only 83 colors, not 256.

The dithering difference

In general, when you index an image with the Adaptive palette and
diffusion dithering, the resulting GIF looks pretty good. Diffusion
dithering creates a smooth, natural-looking gradation between adjacent colors, rather than the sharp contrast between colors (called
banding) that otherwise results. At a distance (or a small size), the
eye merges these dithered patterns into a single color, but viewed
close up (or enlarged), the image appears grainy or speckled.

To see the difference that dithering makes, take a look at Figure 3-2.
On the left, you'll see the image as it looks with dithering, a lovely,
smooth gradation. On the right, is the image saved without dithering:
substantial color banding is evident.

Dithering is not always a boon to mankind. If you have a large
expanse of a flat color, you'll notice white dots where the image has

Figure 3-2. *Dithering turns a heavily banded gradation into a smooth one*

been dithered. Later in this chapter, we'll discuss how to deal with these sorts of images.

To apply the Adaptive palette with diffusion dithering to an RGB image, follow these steps:

1. Open the image, resize it to the actual size you'll use on your web page, and make sure the resolution is set to 72 dpi.

2. Change to Indexed Color mode (Image: Mode: Indexed Color in Photoshop 4.0, and Image: Indexed Color in earlier versions).

3. If your image has 256 or more colors, the default settings will be *Adaptive* for palette, *256* for Colors, *Diffusion* for Dither, and *8bits/pixel* for color depth. If your image has less than 256 colors, the default for palette will be *Exact* and the exact number of colors will be displayed in the Colors field.

4. Click OK to accept these defaults.

Now your image is indexed and ready to be saved in the GIF format.

Reducing color depth

Now you have a good-looking GIF file, but it may be a little larger than you like. One way to decrease file size is to reduce color bit depth.

To understand the importance of color depth, take a look at Figures C-16 to C-19. Figure C-16 is the best quality the GIF format has to offer: 8-bit Adaptive palette, diffusion dither. It looks great (better, in fact, than the original 24-bit image looks on an 8-bit monitor because there are fewer colors to dither). But the file size is 52K: which is too big!

Figure C-17 is the other end of the extreme: at a color depth of 3 bits, the colors are extremely flat and the image has essentially fallen apart, with large areas simply dropping out to white. It's obviously unacceptable, but the file size is a tempting 22K. The right choice is somewhere in the middle.

Many web designers try to keep their bit depth to 5 bits or less, generally a happy medium between file size and quality constraints, primarily to keep their file size small. In this case, a 5-bit palette isn't great, as shown in Figure C-18, but the file size is a reasonable 31K. We're probably not willing to go much higher, but just for kicks, try it at 6 bits. The 6-bit version, shown in Figure C-19, is a *lot* better than the 5-bit version and is only 36K.

Ultimately, you have to decide what file size and image quality you're willing to live with. If you were showing, say, an art portfolio, you'd probably want to err on the side of quality; if this were essentially a decorative image for your page, you'd want to really limit file size. In the previous example, the additional 5K is probably worth the extra quality.

Another way to reduce file size is to turn off dithering. In many cases, this will create unacceptable banding, but not always. Again it depends on the number of colors you're trying to represent.

Saving time with automation

If you've gone through the last section with your own images, you've discovered how time-consuming it can be to convert and save many different versions of your image until you find the perfect balance. If you are using Photoshop 4.0, you can automate the process of applying different color depths and palettes to a single image with Actions.

Take this tip from Sean Parker, the technical wizard at Option X. Sean created an Action, shown in Figure 3-3, that applies the different color depths to the Adaptive palette with diffusion dither, and then applies the Web palette with dither. He has also created an action that applies the different color depths to the adaptive palette with no dither, and then applies the Web palette without dither.

Customizing the Adaptive palette

When Photoshop converts an image from the RGB mode to the Indexed Color mode, it treats all parts of the image equally. It doesn't recognize, for example, that you might be more concerned

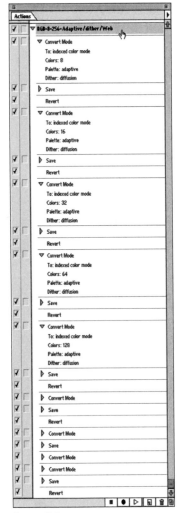

Figure 3-3. *Sean Parker's Action for applying different color depths with diffusion dither*

How big is your image file anyway?

As a creator of web content, you need to pay attention to the file size of your image or graphic. Many web designers have decided that the total size for a web page shouldn't be more than 30K, so every kilobyte counts. How can you determine the actual file size of an image you are currently working on? Unfortunately, Photoshop isn't much help. The size that is displayed on the bottom left of the image window has very little to do with actual number of kilobytes that make up the image. If you are working with a JPEG image, it has nothing to do with the actual compressed file size. (Display the size by positioning the pointer over the triangle in the bottom border, holding down the mouse button, and choosing Document Sizes. These numbers are useful when you want to know the approximate difference in size between a layered and a flattened image. The first value shows the file size of the final file as it would be if its layers were flattened. The second value shows a file size that includes all layers and channels.)

When you choose Image: Image Size, the file size number displayed is only a rough approximation of the actual number of bytes of your image.

To find the actual file size, leave Photoshop and click on your desktop. In Windows, the file size you see in the file list is accurate. On the Mac, however, this number is usually way off. The Macintosh Finder displays not the size of the file but the amount of hard drive space consumed. To find the actual size of a file, use Command/Control-I (or File: Get Info). The first number shown next to Size is the amount of hard drive space the file occupies. The number next to it in parentheses is the more accurate number.

Ultimately, what really matters is the final size of the image file once it is on a web server. This final file size is often much smaller than you think, because unwanted and unneeded data is stripped in the process of putting an image on a server. This is especially true for Macintosh files, because the Mac adds a "resource fork" that is always stripped away by a web server.

about the foreground of the image than the background. But you're not stuck with this situation—you can create a palette that best represents the important parts of your image.

There are at least two ways to do this:

- "Tweak" (or influence) the Adaptive palette
- Create a custom palette

The first way is easier. To tweak the adaptive palette, simply select the area that you want to emphasize with a selection tool. Now when you convert from RGB to Indexed Color mode, Photoshop will automatically weigh the conversion in favor of the selected area.

In Figure C-20, for example, Rebecca's face is the most important element in the image. However, if the Adaptive palette is applied normally to this photograph, too much emphasis will be placed on the colorful background and not enough of the colors that make up the skin tone will be represented. As Figure C-21 shows, the results are not flattering.

But we can tweak the palette by having Photoshop emphasize the colors in the face and de-emphasize the colors in the background. To do this, simply select the face before indexing, as shown in Figure C-22. The new palette, shown in Figure C-23, contains many more of the subtle tonal variations that make the skin tone more realistic.

In the previous example, we got good results by influencing the Adaptive palette. But we could have gotten even better results if we had created a CLUT (Color Look-Up Table) that put total rather than a partial emphasis on the selected area. To do this, you need to create a custom palette. Once you've created this custom palette, you can apply it to your original image or to one comparable in color.

To create a custom palette, follow these steps:

1. Open an RGB image.

2. Make a copy of that image (Image: Duplicate), merging layers if necessary. You'll work on this copy to create the custom palette, then apply the palette to your original.

3. Crop the duplicate image to the most color-critical area. This part of the image will control the color palette.

4. Index this cropped image with the adaptive palette.

5. Save this palette by selecting Image: Mode: Color Table and clicking Save. Give the palette a name and click OK.

Now that we've created a custom palette, we can apply it to the original image. Just index the original and choose Custom palette instead of Adaptive palette. This brings up the Color Table dialog. Click on the Load button and select the custom palette you just created. Photoshop will apply the custom palette to your image.

As you can see in Figure C-24, Rebecca's face is nearly color-perfect. However, since our custom palette doesn't include any colors from the background, the background looks terrible. A solution to this problem would have been to include a few background colors in our custom palette, which could have been done by cropping our image looser.

Using browser-safe colors

So far, we've discussed using the Adaptive palette with dithering to handle continuous-tone images. Now we turn our attention to

images with large areas of flat color. While dithering helps to represent textured images that require more than 256 colors, it creates a
problem for flat colors. If you have an image on a field of blue, for
example, you want to see blue, not a dithered approximation of
blue. For these kinds of images, you should turn dithering off. Typically, you'll index these images with an Exact palette (since it should
have less than 256 colors) and no dither.

Except it's not that simple. Here's why.

One of the web browser's many jobs is to manage color. This is an
issue because web pages typically have numerous images on a
single page, so it would be impossible for an 8-bit system to display
each image's Adaptive palette.

That's why browsers have their own palette, generally known as the
browser-safe palette, shown in Figure C-25. This is a 216-color
palette, the colors of which are common to both Mac and Windows
platforms, shown in Figure C-26. Technically it's called a $6 \times 6 \times 6$
color cube, because the 216 colors are generated by combining just
six colors.

The use of browser-safe colors is an important concept to understand if you want your images and graphics to look their best on the
greatest number of display systems. First of all, if everyone surfing
the Web used a display system capable of displaying millions or
even thousands of colors, we wouldn't need a discussion about
browser-safe colors. There would be plenty of colors to go around.
But the fact is, the majority of Web surfers use 8-bit display systems.

In general, 8-bit Macs use the 256-color system palette, which
contains the 216 browser-safe colors plus 40 more, and Windows
computers always use the browser-safe palette. There do seem to be
times, however, when Macs use the smaller browser-safe palette.

As long as your image contains only the 216 colors in the browser-
safe palette, there's no problem. What happens when your image
contains non-safe colors? The browser either uses dithering to simulate the missing color or it entirely changes the color to one of the
colors in its palette.

Now imagine an image on a blue background. If you pick whatever
blue you want and index with the Exact palette and no dither, do
you get a nice flat color? No, you get dithering, because the browser
will try to approximate the color you asked for from the colors in
the browser palette. No good.

The solution, of course, is to pick a browser-safe blue for that field.
Although you don't have control over what kind of display system

your audience is using, nor do you have control over the way in which a browser dithers or changes colors in your image or graphic, you do have control over which colors you choose to use. When you work with the 216 colors that are common to both the Mac and Windows machines, you can be assured that they will not dither or be replaced by a different color. Of course, these colors may not always look the way that you expect because of individual monitor calibration (or lack of) and the gamma characteristics of various computer platforms—but the differences are relatively predictable.

The best way to use browser-safe colors is to apply them to areas of large expanses of flat colors, while using dithering on areas of continuous tone, subtle gradation, and anti-aliasing.

Photoshop's Web palette

Using Photoshop's Web palette is another quick and easy way to prepare your images and graphics for the GIF format. Using this palette ensures that your image or graphic contains only browser-safe colors.

To apply the Web palette in Photoshop 4.0, index your image as usual, but under the Palette options, choose the Web palette instead of the Adaptive palette. If you're using an earlier version of Photoshop, you'll have to load a Web palette that you've obtained elsewhere (see Appendix B, *Third-Party Software*, for a list of URLs). To do this, choose the Custom palette option and then select the appropriate file from your hard disk. If you don't have a Web palette, you can use the Mac system palette with satisfactory results. This is because the Mac palette contains the 216 browser-safe colors, as well as 40 others.

Again, you need to experiment with your particular image to see if dithering is needed or not.

Replacing non-browser-safe colors

It is not visually pleasing when solid, large expanses of color (such as those found in a background) dither. To avoid this, you can use Photoshop to replace a background or solid color with a browser-safe color, as described in these steps:

1. Open the Swatches palette and choose a browser-safe color from the Web color swatch. (Window: Show Swatches. In Photoshop 3.0: Window: Palettes: Show Swatches.)

2. In the Swatches palette, click on the upper-right pointer, choose Load Swatches from the pull-down menu, and select a browser-safe palette.

Dither last

In general, dithering is quite useful because it optimizes the imaging capability of the hardware. But when resized or otherwise manipulated, a dithered image pixelizes into artificial patterns and clumps. Therefore, before applying a dithering technique, be sure that you have carried out all your other image-processing steps and have correctly sized the image.

3. Use the Eyedropper tool and fill the foreground box with the browser-safe color.

4. Use either Photoshop's Magic Wand or manual selection tools to select the area of the image that you want to change. You could also use the Color Range tool.

    (If you use the Magic Wand tool, be sure to experiment with the Grow and Similar commands found under the Select menu. These options are especially useful to isolate large expanses of background or areas of similar color.)

5. Fill the selected area with the color that you chose from the browser-safe palette.

Reducing colors

Once you apply the Web palette in Photoshop, you end up with an indexed image that contains 216 browser-safe colors. But what if you don't need 216 colors? What if your image contains only 64 colors, or, for that matter, 16? By saving your file with 216 colors you have created an unnecessarily large file. What to do now? You can get rid of the unused colors by following these steps:

1. Switch to RGB mode.

2. Without doing anything else, switch back to Indexed Color mode. If your image has less than 216 colors, the Exact palette should be selected, and the number of colors in the image will be displayed.

3. Click OK and save the indexed image as a GIF.

The new image will look exactly the same as the original, while the file size will shrink.

Selective dithering

When you command Photoshop to dither an image, it applies the dither pattern to the entire image, even to areas that you might not want to dither such as areas containing flat colors. Wouldn't it be great if you could "tell" Photoshop to selectively dither a small part of an image and yet keep the other parts intact?

c|net's Casey Caston has found a way to do just that. To use Caston's method of selective dithering, follow these steps:

1. In RGB mode, copy the part of the image to dither.

2. Index the image.

3. Paste the copied portion back from the Clipboard to the indexed but undithered image. Photoshop automatically dithers the pasted RGB selection, leaving the rest of the image untouched.

Caston regularly uses this technique to give him very specific control over the way his c|net graphics look.

The next three color figures show the results of this approach to indexing a GIF. Figure C-27 shows the graphic indexed to the Web palette. Figure C-28 shows the image with the adaptive palette. And Figure C-29 shows the results of the combination approach: some of the image is dithered, some isn't.

Getting better tiled backgrounds

When an image or graphic is used as the background for a web page, you have to be especially careful to use browser-safe colors. This is because browsers handle background images differently than other images. When it comes to backgrounds, the browser will shift non-browser-safe colors instead of dithering them.

This became quite apparent to designer Gregg Hartling of Venu communications when he tried to use a GIF background tile that he had created using the Adaptive palette. Gregg knew that by using the Adaptive palette he ran the risk of introducing colors that weren't browser-safe. He thought the image might dither when displayed on an 8-bit system, but he didn't see that as a problem because the dither would add a nice effect to the image.

But the background GIF didn't dither. Instead, as you can see in Figure C-30, the browser substituted colors from the Web palette and that's all it did. The result was a clumpy, banding-like effect. Gregg quickly went back to his original image and used the browser-safe palette with diffusion dither selected and got the results he wanted, as shown in Figure C-31.

A little more work

As you've seen in this chapter, indexing a graphic in preparation for the GIF file format takes a bit of work, expecially if you are trying to get it completely right. Remember, what may seem daunting at first becomes easier and easier as you become familiar with the various Photoshop settings and how they affect different types of images and graphics. In the next chapter, we'll show you ways to maintain even more control over the color in your graphics by using browser-safe colors from the start.

CHAPTER FOUR

CREATING GIFS FROM SCRATCH

As discussed in the last chapter, when you use Photoshop to create web graphics and illustrations, it's a good idea to keep the limitations of the Web in mind from the onset. Basically, this means using the browser-safe 216-color palette.

By using these 216 colors and saving your final work in the GIF file format, you can be assured that your work will not dither or otherwise change when viewed on an 8-bit display system. By using just the necessary amount of color, you can also be sure, that your file size is as small as possible so that your image will download quickly.

Although 216 colors may not sound like a lot of color, web designers have not only learned to live with this limited palette, but have also found ways to create beautiful and effective work—in spite of its limitations. In this chapter, you'll see how they do it. You'll also learn how to create so-called hybrid browser-safe colors that extend the number of web-safe colors well beyond 216, as well as how to borrow color swatches from other web graphics.

In this chapter

- From RGB to indexed color
- Controlling anti-aliasing with custom brushes
- Working in Indexed Color mode
- Creating an illusion of translucency
- Hijacking a color palette
- Creating your own browser-safe colors
- On to transparency

From RGB to indexed color

Corey Hitchcock is an illustrator/designer who works at The Gate, the online service of the *San Francisco Chronicle* and *Examiner.* The web site is updated hourly, and because of the hectic schedule, Corey has quickly gotten to know the ins and outs of the Web. She knows, for example, that by working directly from the browser-safe palette, her graphics will look the way she wants on the largest number of monitors.

She works in Photoshop's RGB mode, which gives her the advantage of all of Photoshop's filters, plug-ins, and layer features; however, in

Locating a swatch

In order to load a brows-
er-safe swatch, open the
Swatches palette. *Photo-
shop 4.0*: Window: Show
Swatches. *Photoshop 3.0*:
Window: Palettes: Show
Swatches. In the Switch-
es palette, click on the upper-right pointer and
choose Load Swatches
from the pull-down
menu. Photoshop 4.0 has
included a Web palette in
its Goodies folder. Select
and choose this file now
or select and load anoth-
er browser-safe swatch
that you've acquired.

this mode there is always a chance that she might introduce non-
browser-safe colors into her work. As a result, when she is finished,
and when she is ready to convert her work to the Index mode so it
can be saved as a GIF, she applies Photoshop 4.0's Web palette.

Figure C-32 shows one of her creations, a colored dragon that was
part of a feature on the Chinese new year.

To create the image with browser-safe colors:

1. She loaded a palette of browser-safe colors into her Swatches
   palette. Corey works with a special color palette that is organized by hue and value.

2. She scanned and opened a line drawing that she made of a
   dragon.

3. She created a new layer.

4. In the new layer, she used the Selection tool to roughly outline
   the edges of the dragon.

5. She chose a browser-safe red from the Swatches palette as the
   background color. Then she chose a browser-safe orange and
   made it the foreground color.

6. She used the Gradient tool to fill the selection in the new layer,
   as shown in Figure C-33. (Remember that the Gradient tool adds
   additional colors to create the blend between these two colors.
   The more variations between the two colors, the more non-
   browser-safe colors will be introduced.)

7. She chose Overlay from the Layers pull-down menu so that the
   gradated colors would blend nicely with the line drawing.

8. She converted her RGB file to the Indexed Color mode, using
   the Web palette. (Because the Gradient tool added a few non-
   browser-safe colors, there was a slight change between the RGB
   and the indexed versions.)

In a very short time, Corey created an illustration that not only
embellishes a Gate web page, but at 15K also loads fast and looks
the same regardless of the monitor it is viewed on.

Controlling anti-aliasing with custom brushes

Every two weeks, Discovery's Brian Frick creates an illustration for a
column called "The Skinny On." Like Corey Hitchcock, Brian works
in Photoshop's RGB mode and uses browser-safe color swatches.
Most often, he uses Photoshop's Paintbrush tool, but he creates and
uses custom brushes that reduce the chance of non-browser-safe
colors being introduced through anti-aliasing.

The only Photoshop tool that doesn't automatically anti-alias—and therefore add unwanted, non-browser-safe colors—is the Pencil tool. But the Pencil tool creates a very hard, jagged edge that Brian rarely uses. The custom brushes that he makes create a look between the hard edge of the Pencil tool and the normally soft edge of the Paintbrush. Figure 4-1 shows some of the custom brushes he created. The illustrations for "The Skinny On" were created using these custom brushes.

The illustrations are also built layer by layer, as shown in Figure C-34. Brian prefers working this way so that he can easily edit any specific part of the illustration at any time.

To create the custom brushes and the toilet bowl illustration, Brian followed these steps:

1. He created a new file with a white background, and then loaded the browser-safe palette.

2. He created a new layer and used a custom brush to paint the browser-safe green background.

   To make the custom brush, he did the following:

   a. He created a new 100 × 100 pixel file with a white background that he immediately converted to grayscale mode.

   b. He chose one of the non-blurred medium-sized brush shapes from the Brushes palette and dabbed a gray spot onto the white background. (Upon magnification, a soft edge on this gray dab is noticeable, a result of the paintbrush automatically anti-aliasing.)

   c. He increased the contrast of the paint dab by 60% (Image: Adjust: Brightness/Contrast). This made the edge "harder" and reduced the chance of non-browser-safe colors being introduced when Brian used the paintbrush.

   d. He selected the paint dab using the rectangular Selection tool, and back in his original file containing the toilet bowl, he opened his Brushes palette and chose Define Brush from the pull-down menu. This loaded the new shape into the palette window, ready to be used in this illustration and others.

3. He created a new layer and drew the lime-green vertical lines. Again, he used the custom brush to create the bold vertical lines. To create the dotted lines, he used the same brush, but altered it by double-clicking on the brush shape in the Brush palette window, and setting the spacing to 190.

   (Whenever Brian finishes with a layer, he selects Preserve Transparency in the Layers palette window. This way he saves the

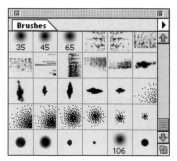

Figure 4-1. *Brian Frick's Brushes palette shows some of his custom brushes*

Losing color values

Keep in mind that when you convert from one color mode to another, as Corey Hitchcock did, you've created a permanent change to the color values of the image. When you go from RGB to Index and then back to RGB, the color values that were lost when indexed in the first place are never replaced just by going back to the RGB space. For this reason, it is advisable always to save a copy of the original RGB version.

Also keep in mind that converting to Index color always flattens the layers of an image. If you want to edit the original version with the layers intact, be sure to save a copy of your image before indexing the color.

shape of the drawing, but if he wants, he can go back and change the color.)

4. In other layers, Brian made the flowers and the toilet bowl, again using the paintbrush and the brush tip that he created. He almost always uses the Paintbrush tool, although sometimes when he wants to add shades of color, he will use the Airbrush or Dodge/Burn tools—which he did with the toilet bowl itself.

5. He converted his illustration to Indexed Color mode, applying Photoshop's Web palette. (In some cases, he applies the Adaptive palette. For example, he did this with the peanut illustration shown in Figure 4-2, because he wanted to preserve the peanut's subtle shades of brown, which were not browser-safe. When he applied the Adaptive palette to the peanut illustration, however, the green background (which was browser-safe) shifted. He then had to go back to the illustration, select the now non-browser-safe green, fill it with browser-safe green, then reconvert his illustration once again to the Index mode. This time, the Exact palette was automatically selected. When the peanut illustration is seen on an 8-bit monitor, the brown dithers, but the background looks fine. When it is viewed on systems with a greater color capability, everything looks fine.)

Every two weeks Brian Frick paints a new illustration with browser-safe colors for Discovery's "The Skinny On" section.

Working in Indexed Color mode

Designer Valerie Stambaugh likes a challenge, but that's not the reason she chose Photoshop's Indexed Color mode to create a self-portrait for her web page, as shown in Figure C-35. None of Photoshop's filters, plug-ins, or multilayer capabilities is available in the Index mode (drawing tools and some selection tools are available, however), but by working in Indexed Color mode, Valerie is guaranteed that her work contains only browser-safe colors. By controlling the exact number of colors that she used, she also created an image with a very small file size.

This is how she created the self-portrait:

1. She created a new RGB file, 200 × 200 pixels.

2. She changed mode from RGB to Indexed Color. In the Indexed Color dialog box, she chose Web palette and turned off dithering.

3. She loaded the browser-safe palette in the Swatches palette.

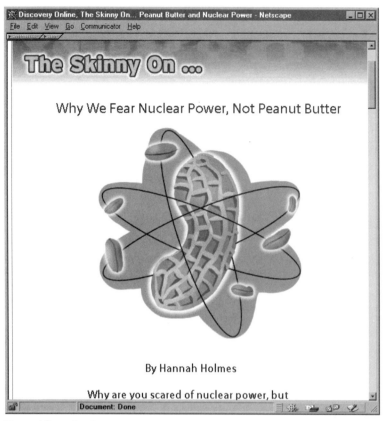

Figure 4-2. *"The Skinny On" section featuring another of Brian Frick's illustrations*

4. She filled the background with a blue from the browser-safe swatch.

5. To create the rounded, pea-green box, she made a rectangular selection and feathered the selection 10 pixels (Select: Feather).

6. To paint with the browser-safe colors in the Swatches palette, she clicked on a desired color, making it Photoshop's foreground color and painted with the Pencil and Brush tools. (She compares the process of "dipping" into the color palette and then painting to watercolor painting.) Painting in stages, she first applied the background, then built her drawing up step by step, each stroke applied on top of the previous one.

7. When she was finished, Valerie briefly switched back to the RGB mode. Because she had worked with fewer than 216 colors, the Exact palette was automatically selected when she went back to Indexed Color mode. Photoshop created a color look-up table containing only the colors in the self-portrait, keeping her file size down to a minimum.

Creating an illusion of translucency

Undaunted by the restrictions imposed on her by working in Indexed Color mode, Valerie Stambaugh figured out a way to create an illusion of translucency, as shown in Figures C-36 and C-37. This is a simple task when you have the benefits of layers, but to do this in Indexed Color mode, you have to rely on visual trickery.

Valerie created a transparent effect in Photoshop 4.0 by following these steps:

1. She created a new 200 × 200-pixel file in Indexed Color mode with a white background.

2. She made and filled a circle with a browser-safe yellow with the circular selection tool. (To create a perfect circle, hold down the Shift key while using the circular Selection tool.)

3. She dragged the still-active circular selection completely to the right of the now-yellow circle.

4. She filled this selection with a browser-safe blue. At this point she had a yellow circle on the left and a blue circle on the right.

5. She dragged the still-active circular selection to the left until it was almost off the blue circle, leaving a crescent area of the blue circle selected. She then deselected the white and yellow areas outside of the selected blue area by Option/Alt-clicking with the Magic Wand. When she was finished, only the crescent area of the blue circle was selected.

6. She then filled this selection with a browser-safe green. She used the Magic Wand to add the rest of the blue circle to the selection, as shown in Figure C-36. With the Move tool, she dragged the now blue and green circle to meet the yellow circle, giving the illusion of a blending of the two colors, as shown in Figure C-37.

Hijacking a color palette

It's difficult to get web designers to admit it, but many of them often "borrow" color palettes from other web sites.

If you want to "hijack" a color palette, and you don't have a moral problem with it, first save the GIF to your system. In most browsers, you can place your cursor over the illustration or graphic you want, and click and hold (Mac) or right-click (Windows) to bring up a pop-up menu that lets you save the file. (There is no point in trying to hijack the colors contained in a JPEG image. JPEG images are not indexed and don't contain a color look-up table.)

Then open the graphic in Photoshop. Because the image is already indexed, you will be able to view its CLUT by selecting Image: Mode: Color Table. All the colors found in the image will show up in the color palette, as shown in Figure 4-3. Save this palette by choosing the Save button. Don't publish the image without getting permission, but the colors are now yours.

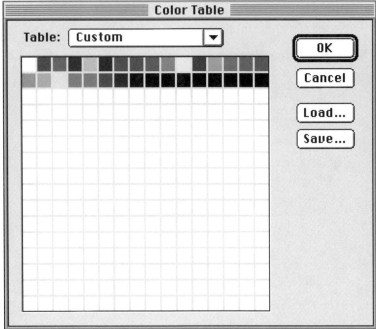

Figure 4-3. *Selecting Image: Mode: Color Table will display the palette of the image, and clicking on the Save button saves the palette for use with other images*

You can either apply this custom palette directly to an existing image (index the image, choose the Custom palette, and click the Load button to load your hijacked palette) or open the palette in the Swatches palette and use any of Photoshop's tools to paint, airbrush, fill, or draw with a color selected from the swatch.

Creating your own browser-safe colors

There are 216 colors that have been designated as browser-safe. These are the colors that won't dither or be exchanged when they are viewed on an 8-bit monitor regardless of the computer platform used.

However, you can create your own "hybrid" browser-safe colors and extend the number of safe colors well beyond 216. You can load these hybrid colors in your Swatches palette and paint or draw with them as you would any color. You can also fill selections with them by using the Photoshop's Fill command.

The principle of hybrid colors is similar to that of dithering: by choosing two or more colors and arranging them in a pattern, you can simulate the effect of a new, third color. Because you use only browser-safe colors to start, the third color will also be browser-safe.

The 4-pixel method

Here's what Brian Frick did to create a hybrid color, which he used in the background for the Discovery Online page:

1. He started by creating a new file of 2 × 2 pixels (72 dpi).

2. Then he set the Pencil tool to be 1-pixel wide.

3. He loaded a browser-safe swatch and chose a color. He used his 1-pixel pencil tip to place this color in the top-left and bottom-right pixels. He chose another browser-safe color from the swatches and filled the remaining pixels with this color, as shown in Figure C-38.

4. He selected Edit: Define Pattern. To fill a selection with this color, he selected an area, selected Edit: Fill, and chose Pattern in the Fill dialog box. This filled the area with the hybrid color.

Brian has created several hybrid colors this way, and saved them in a custom swatch that he can access at any time.

The linear-stripe method

New York designer Tom Walker created his hybrid browser-safe colors a bit differently than Brian Frick, but his results are just as useful. As shown in Figure C-39, Tom created hybrid colors by filling 2-pixel-wide horizontal selections with browser-safe colors.

The random noise method

Tom used Photoshop's Add Noise filter to apply random noise to a selection of browser-safe colors, as shown in Figure C-40. To make sure that he hadn't introduced any unsafe web colors, he indexed his work using the browser-safe palette.

On to transparency

Now that you've learned to use Photoshop both to convert existing graphics into the GIF file format and to create graphics from scratch using the browser-safe palette, it's time to move on to the next chapter, where you'll learn how to use Photoshop and its GIF89a export module. With this module, you'll be able to take all those beautiful GIF images and graphics that you've just created, designate specific areas as transparent, and make them pop dynamically from the electronic page. Onwards!

SPECIAL EFFECTS WITH TRANSPARENT GIFs

With the GIF89a Export module, Photoshop has become one of the best ways to create transparent GIFs. Not only does Photoshop make it easy to make a single color transparent, but it is now also easy to make whole areas of an image transparent—no matter how many colors they contain. To access the GIF89a Export module, select File: Export: GIF89a.

Figure 5-1 illustrates how awkward graphics can look on a web page without the benefit of Photoshop's most powerful web tool, the GIF89a Export module.

In Figure 5-2, the graphics blend seamlessly into the background, creating a clean and professional-looking page. The difference is transparency. That's why the GIF89a format is so important for web designers. And with Photoshop's GIF89a Export module, Photoshop is now one of the best tools for creating transparent GIFs.

There are three ways to use the GIF89a Export Module, described in the following list. Each method provides an appropriate solution for a variety of situations:

- *Color-based transparency.* In Indexed Color mode, export the image and choose one or several colors to be transparent. This is the fastest and easiest method.

- *Selection-based transparency.* In RGB mode, create a mask and then export the image. The masked parts of the image will be transparent, regardless of the colors they contain. Although this method requires more work, it also offers the most control over how and where the transparency is applied.

- *Layers-based transparency.* In a Photoshop file, export one or more layers as separate transparent GIFs. Any transparent pixels

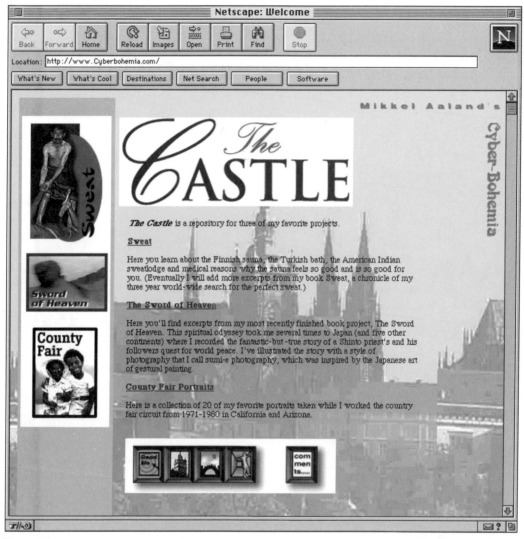

Figure 5-1. *Without transparency, graphics are rectangular and don't blend with page backgrounds*

in the layer will be transparent in the exported GIF. This method is particularly useful if you are using Photoshop as a web layout tool.

The color method: quick and easy

Depending on which color mode you're in, you'll get a different GIF89a Export dialog. For this first method, let's assume you're working in Indexed Color mode, as Valerie Stambaugh and I did for

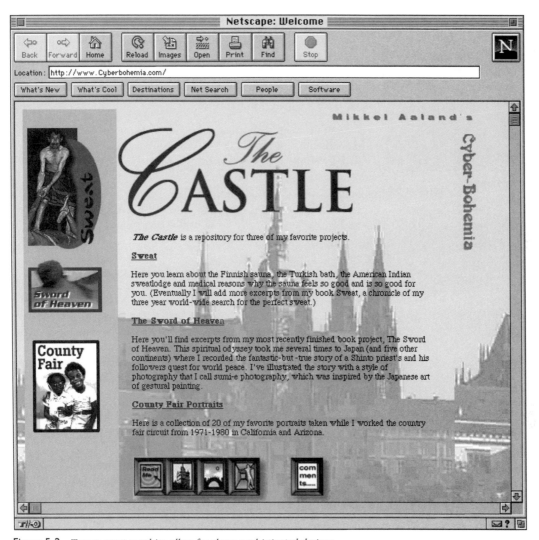

Figure 5-2. *Transparent graphics allow for clean, sophisticated designs*

the Sword of Heaven icon for my web site, Cyber-Bohemia. We created this graphic on a one-color background, and didn't use this color in the image itself. Exporting the graphic to GIF89a brings up the Export dialog box shown in Figure C-41.

A preview of the image appears in the top left of the dialog box. At the bottom is a palette of all the colors used in the image. To the right are a number of options and tools, including an eyedropper tool, a move tool (the hand), and a zoom tool. The eyedropper is used to select colors to be transparent, the hand positions the image in the preview window, and the magnifying glass zooms into the

Getting the module

The GIF89a Export module is included with Photoshop 4.0 and with some later versions of Photoshop 3.0. You must have version 3.01 or later to use the module. If you don't have it, you can download it for free from Adobe's web site (*www.adobe.com*). Once you've downloaded it, place it in the *Plug-ins* folder within your *Photoshop* folder.

image. Above these tools is a color swatch labeled "Transparency Index Color" (we'll get to that shortly).

It's very simple to make the gold background transparent. With the eyedropper tool selected, click anywhere in the gold background area. All the gold in the image turns gray, indicating that it is now transparent, as shown in Figure C-42.

If you want to make additional colors transparent, hold down the Shift key and click on other colors in the image. Alternatively, you can click or Shift-click on the color palette at the bottom to select colors for transparency. You can deselect a color by pressing Command/Control and clicking the color again. Before you click OK, you can restore all the original colors at any time by pressing the Option/Alt key (which changes the Cancel button to a Reset button) and clicking Reset.

Changing the default transparency color

There may be times when you don't want Photoshop to display transparent areas as gray. If your image contains gray, for instance, it may be confusing for gray to be the transparent color. You can select any color you want to indicate transparency; it doesn't really matter. To change the transparent index color to red, for example, just click on the color swatch to bring up Photoshop's color picker and select a different color. You can change the transparency index color only after you've made a transparent color selection.

It's worth understanding what this "transparent index" stuff is all about. While Photoshop presents the color palette of an image as something visual, in the actual GIF file the palette, or index, is a bunch of numbers with colors assigned to them. Rather than thinking about the specific colors in an image, the GIF file thinks in terms of index numbers. Each index number has a color value associated with it. For example, the value of 1 might be 60,20,255; the value of 2 might be 125,0,255; and so on. (The color value numbers represent RGB values.)

So a GIF file actually associates index numbers (not absolute color values) with each pixel in the image: this pixel is color 0, this pixel is color 1, and so on. (Actually, GIF compresses images by not repeating data for every single pixel; when contiguous pixels have the same value, the index is just given once.)

So how is transparency defined in a GIF file? A transparency flag is assigned to one index number. If the gold color in the previous example were color 0 in the index, then that number would be flagged as transparent. The important point is that the index, not the actual color, defines transparency.

You can actually see this designated color if you open a GIF89a image and look at its CLUT (Image: Mode: Color Table). The color will usually be in the first or last position of the CLUT. You might also notice elsewhere in the CLUT a color that looks exactly the same. Because GIF is an indexed color format, it's entirely possible to have two index numbers with the exact same color value—but only one will be transparent.

When the color method doesn't work

The color-based method won't work if your background color is found elsewhere in the image. For example, I indexed a navigation bar from the Castle web page, choosing the Adaptive palette and diffusion dither because I wanted to maintain the soft shadows. I then ran the GIF89a Export module and began selecting colors with the Eyedropper tool. Because the graphic contained some of the same colors found in the background, I ran into trouble, as shown in Figure C-43. Part of the graphic itself turned red, meaning it had become transparent. Placed on a web page, critical parts of the graphic would disappear. Oops.

So what's the solution for this color-bleeding effect? There are a couple of different approaches for making the background transparent but preserving the image:

- Change the background color
- Mask off the image

Preventing unwanted color bleeding

In many cases, there's a simple workaround for the color-bleeding problem described above: just change the background color to some color not found in the image. That way, when the background color goes transparent, the image will remain intact. (This method is insufficient for anti-aliased images and those that contain features like drop shadows. In these images, selecting a single background color as transparent results in a "halo" effect. Solutions for this problem are discussed later in this chapter.)

Luke Knowland of HotWired used this idea to produce a striking graphic for HotWired's Web Monkey site, shown in Figure C-44. Because he created a colored tint not found in other parts of the image, there is no bleeding of the transparency effect into unwanted parts of the image. Luke's original image of Wendy Owen was taken with a Kodak DC-50 digital camera.

Keep in mind that Luke's method is useful only if you work with an image or graphic that lends itself to tinting.

Determining the GIF version

The GIF89a Export module lets you specify transparency in your GIF. When you don't care about transparency, you can simply select File: Save, File: Save As or File: Save a Copy and specify CompuServe GIF from the format pop-up menu. In Photoshop 3.0, doing this saved the older GIF87a format, which doesn't support transparency. In Photoshop 4.0, the File operations save a GIF89a file.

How do you know which GIF format your version of Photoshop has written? A simple way is to open your GIF file within a program such as Microsoft Word. The text that appears is mostly garbage, but before the mess, at the top of the document, you will see either the letters GIF89a or GIF87a, which identify exactly what kind of GIF you are using.

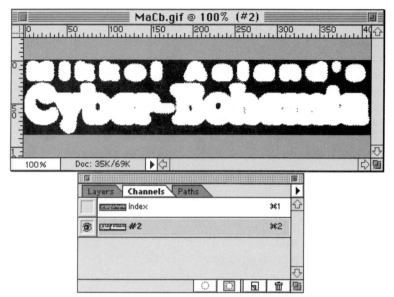

Figure 5-3. *When you open a GIF89a with a transparent color in Photoshop 4.0,*
an editable mask appears in the Channels palette

Channel power: editing transparent areas

Here's one of the coolest things about creating and editing transparent GIFs in Photoshop 4.0.
When you open a GIF89a file (whether it was created in Photoshop or some other application),
check the Channels palette. You'll see that Photoshop creates a channel mask of the transparent
areas, as shown in Figure 5-3. This is a very powerful feature because it lets you add to or subtract
from the transparent area by using standard painting and drawing tools.

You can also use channel masks instead of colors to define transparency from the get-go. See the
later section "Working with masks."

To edit the transparent area, follow these steps:

1. In Photoshop 4.0 or higher, open your GIF89a file. If it contains a transparent area or color,
    you will see the "mask" by viewing the Channels palette.

2. Open the channel containing the mask. You can add to the mask and therefore to the trans-
    parent areas by painting or airbrushing dark colors, and subtract from the mask by adding
    lighter colors or erasing.

3. When you save, these new transparency settings will be applied.

Here are the steps Luke took to create this graphic:

1. Opening the image in Photoshop 3.05, he used the Hue/Saturation dialog (Image: Adjust: Hue/Saturation) to desaturate the image until it was essentially a monotone image. Since that made the image quite flat, he boosted the brightness and contrast (Image: Adjust: Brightness/Contrast).

2. He created a new layer and filled it with pure blue (Red=0, Green=0, Blue=255). This blue will tint his monotone image and provide a color absent from the live image.

3. He made another new layer and pasted in a template with an orange background that he'd made, containing an oval shape with the letters *webmo*, as shown in Figure C-44.

4. To blend the two layers, he selected Difference in the Layers palette blending pop-up menu. Using the Opacity slider, he chose 100%.

5. He changed modes to Indexed Color (Image: Mode: Indexed Color), flattened the layers, and selected Adaptive palette with no dither.

6. In the GIF89a Export module, he clicked the Eyedropper tool on the orange color he wanted to be transparent, confident that the orange color was absent from the blue-tinted photograph of Wendy. Figure 5-4 shows the (black) area that would be masked out or transparent.

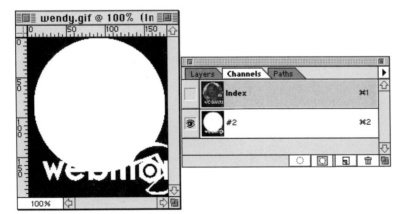

Figure 5-4. *The black defines the area to be transparent*

7. He clicked OK and saved the file. Figure 5-5 shows the final image on the web page.

Saving photos as GIFs

This chapter has several examples of photos saved as GIFs, rather than JPEGs. There are times when you should choose to save a photograph in the GIF format, especially if you want to utilize the handy GIF89a transparency feature.

Just keep in mind that saving a photo in the GIF format means two things: first, you won't be able to achieve the smallest possible file size, and second, you'll have only 256 shades of gray or color to work with.

Although you can still get good results, you'll need to experiment. Some photos look good only if you use the Adaptive palette and diffusion dither. Sometimes you'll need to tweak the Adaptive palette, and sometimes, especially with monotone photos, you can use a browser-safe palette with no diffusion and get good results.

Fast merging

For a quick way to merge layers, in the Layers palette, hold down Option/ Alt while clicking on the line between the two layers.

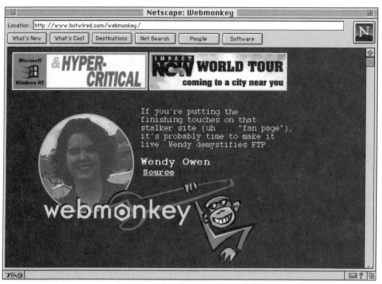

Figure 5-5. *The completed web page, with none of the orange appearing in it*

Working with masks

There are times when applying a mask is the best way to go when you want to add transparent areas to your graphic. This is my favorite method to create transparent GIFs, but it requires an understanding of Photoshop's powerful masking capabilities.

Let's go back to the problem we had in our earlier example of the navigational graphic, described in "When the color method doesn't work." The image contained the same color as the background. Selecting the background color as transparent also made those portions of the image transparent. One way to avoid this would be to select a different color (one not found in the image), but this is insufficient for antialiased images.

By creating a Photoshop mask, however, we could have controlled the *area* of transparency instead of the color. This, in effect, would protect our graphic and keep it intact, but make the areas outside of it go away or become transparent.

To create a mask that protects specific parts of your image, you can:

- Make a selection, either with selection tools or the Color Range dialog (Select: Color Range) and save it as a channel (Select: Save Selection).

- Make a selection and then create a Quick Mask.

Masks appear in the Channels palette where you can edit them at any time.

Applying masks with GIF89a

Once you've created your transparency mask, apply it to your image in the GIF89a Export module by selecting it from the Transparency From pull-down menu, as shown in Figure 5-6. In this example, the mask is identified as *Quick Mask*. The name you'll see will be whatever you've called the channel that contains the mask.

When you choose a channel from the Transparency From menu, the GIF89a Export module automatically applies the mask to your image, making the masked areas transparent. In the preview window, you'll see exactly how the mask is applied.

Selecting transparency via masks instead of colors offers much more control over transparency in GIF images. Once you get the hang of it, you'll be hooked.

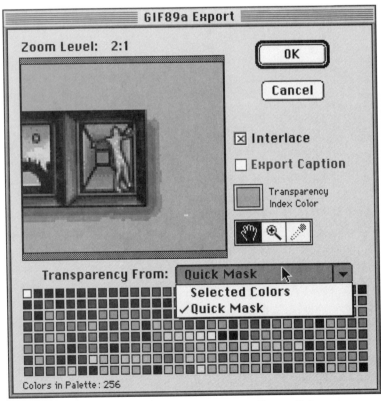

Figure 5-6. *Masks can be selected in the Transparency From pull-down menu*

> **Variable opacity: not an option in GIF89a**
>
> A Photoshop mask consists of 8 bits of information and is capable of variable transparency. You can apply a gray or other neutral color and create a semitransparent mask, resulting in just a portion of the background color showing through. By this means, you can achieve all those visually pleasing effects such as smooth, multitonal transitions between visible and invisible areas like those associated with such effects as feathering and anti-aliasing.
>
> On the other hand, the GIF89a format supports only one transparent color, which effectively means a 1-bit mask. Variable opacity is not an option with the GIF89a format. Areas are either transparent or not.

Going for speed and control

Photoshop wizard Brian Frick efficiently used the masking technique to create a smart-looking page for a Discovery story on computer hackers, shown in Figure C-45. (Pay particular attention to step 7, where Brian quickly creates a mask from a transparent layer. Learning shortcuts such as this one will improve the ease and productivity with which you create transparent GIFs.)

Figure 5-7. *Brian created the text and graphics by hand, then scanned them and filled them with color in Photoshop*

Brian began by drawing the illustrations on paper, as shown in Figure 5-7, and then scanned them as 1-bit graphics.

1. In Photoshop, he selected the white background area with the Magic Wand, and deleted it, leaving only the black outlines of the letters against a now-transparent background.

2. To make his graphics look chunky and fit the spirit of the story, he clicked the Paint Bucket and turned off Anti-alias in the Paint Bucket Options palette.

3. He filled the letters with browser-safe colors.

4. He opened a separate file that contained the background.

5. He selected and copied the "hackers" graphic.

6. With the two files open, he pasted the graphic file into the background file. This created a new layer in the background file. He named the graphic layer *screen* and the background layer *Pattern*. (By selecting the illustration and placing it against the busy background, Brian was able to visually inspect the relationship between the illustration and the background, a valuable step in ascertaining the overall effectiveness of his work.)

7. To quickly create a channel mask, he held down the Command/
    Control key and clicked on the *screen* layer in the Layers
    palette. Presto! This instantly selected the graphics on that layer,
    and he saved the selection, thus creating a mask. In Figure 5-8,
    the mask appears as channel #4 in the Channels palette.

8. Then he merged the two layers and indexed the image with the
    Web palette, no dither.

9. To reduce the number of colors in the file, he converted back to
    RGB mode, then indexed the image again, this time selecting
    the Exact palette. This reduced the number of colors from 216 to
    29, reducing the file size.

10. He exported the image to GIF89a, selecting channel #4 as his
    mask to make the background transparent, shown in Figure 5-9.

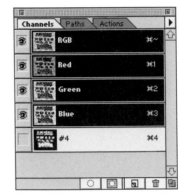

Figure 5-8. *The mask in channel #4 becomes available as a transparency mask in the GIF89a Export module*

Figure 5-9. *Selecting transparency from a mask within the GIF89a Export module*

Exactly the effect he was looking for! He then went back and
performed the same process on the two remaining parts of the
graphic.

The dreaded halo syndrome

In the previous example, Brian worked with aliased graphics to achieve a particular, but often unwanted, hard-edged effect. But what happens when we apply a mask to anti-aliased text, or to a graphic with a soft drop shadow, such as the navigation bar for the Castle page we looked at earlier? If you're not careful, you'll end up with the dreaded halo effect—a colored edge around the image, which you'll see if you skip ahead to Figure 5-12.

The following step-by-step example describes how I created and edited a Quick Mask, and applied the mask to the navigational bar using the GIF89a Export module. Although I created a graphic that "floats" on a web page, I lost the smooth look of the drop shadow because I didn't take into account the halo effect.

Here's what I did:

1. I selected the navigation bar.

2. I clicked the Quick Mask icon at the bottom of the Toolbox, turning the selection into a Quick Mask, which appears in the Channels palette, as shown in Figure 5-10.

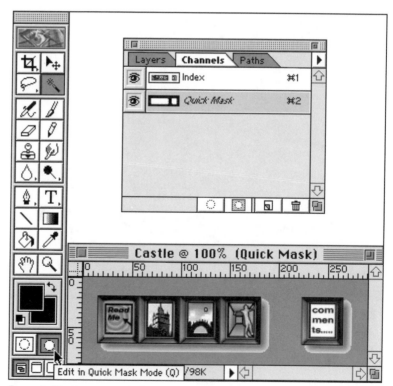

Figure 5-10. *First create a selection*

I didn't make any changes to the mask, but at this point, one can edit the mask with the Airbrush, Paintbrush, Selection, or Eraser tools. To add to the mask, use colors as dark as or darker than the mask. To subtract from the mask, use colors lighter than the mask.

3.   I switched to Indexed Color mode and then ran the GIF Export module. (You must be in Indexed Color mode to use quick masks with the GIF module.)

4.   In the dialog, I selected Quick Mask from the Transparency From pop-up menu and clicked OK (see Figure 5-11). Figure 5-12 shows the problematic result.

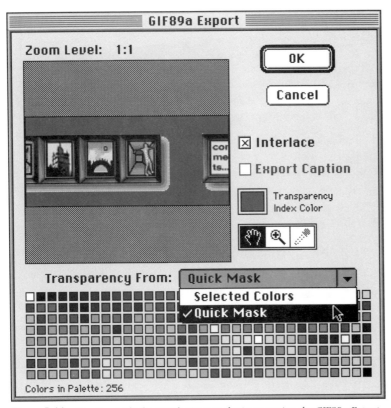

Figure 5-11. *Finally, apply the Quick Menu to the image using the GIF89a Export module*

So how could I have avoided the halo effect and kept the gradual tonal transition of the drop shadow? There are a couple of solutions to the halo problem. First, you can avoid using anti-aliased text or graphics like Brian did. This is fine for certain graphics and small

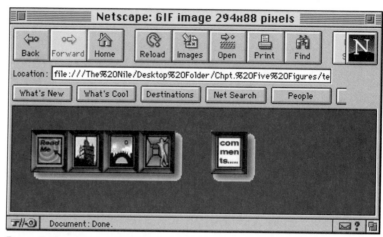

Figure 5-12. *The dreaded "halo" effect*

text that you want to appear crisp and readable. But for most graphics and larger text this isn't a practical solution. The jagged edge of aliasing can be distracting unless it is deliberately used for a special effect (as in Brian's case).

The real solution is to produce your graphic against the background color you'll use on your page. When you place the graphic on the page, the anti-aliasing blends with the background, resulting in a halo-free page. If you have a multicolor background, you can use a dominant color from your background. The next two sections explain how to do this.

Using the same color background

A simple and practical solution to these limitations of GIF89a is to create your graphic against the background color of your web page. When you create a mask, don't mask out the soft edges of your text or any shadows that you want to retain. It doesn't matter if you pick up some of the background color because the colors will blend when the graphic is placed against the web page of the same color.

This is what I did to get the effect shown in Figure 5-13. I followed the same procedures outlined above to create and apply a Quick mask to my navigational bar, except *this* time, I began by placing my navigational bar on the web page background image.

This method works best when your background is a single color. If your background contains many colors, you'll need to use the next method.

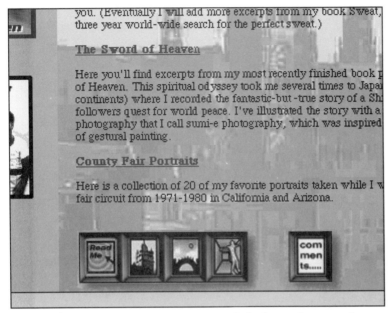

Figure 5-13. *This time I placed my icon against the background image and maintained the soft drop-shadow look*

Preserving an anti-aliased look with a multicolored background

For a Discovery story on tornadoes, our man Brian Frick has found yet another technique to avoid unwanted halos and keep the soft, anti-aliased look even when the background is multicolored. The key here is Brian's choice of a dominant color from the cascade of colored strips that make up his background.

1. He began by selecting a dominant color from his web page's multicolored, tiled background.

2. He then created a new file and filled a background layer with that color.

3. He placed anti-aliased text on top of the color and indexed the image. After experimenting with different color-depth options, he finally chose the Adaptive palette and 7-bit color depth with diffusion dither.

4. Finally, he selected the background of the image as a transparent color. This drops out not only the background of the image but also some colors in the type, as shown in Figure C-46. But here's the thing: it doesn't matter. When the graphic is placed on the web page, the missing color is supplied by the page's background.

5. As shown in Figure C-47, Brian successfully maintained the anti-aliased look that he set out to achieve.

Transparency direct from layers

A third method of creating transparent areas or colors requires that you target one or more specific transparent Photoshop layers and export those layers directly into the GIF89a Export module. When you apply the GIF89a Export module, all the areas that were transparent in your layers will remain transparent when you open your graphic on a web background.

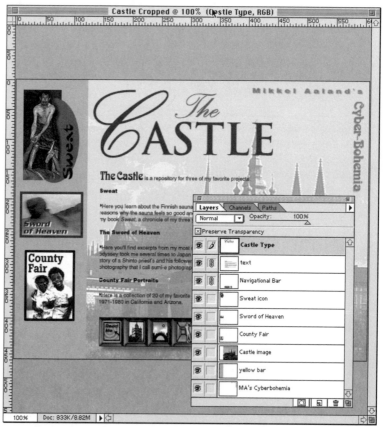

Figure 5-14. *To use the layer method to create a transparent area, start by targeting the layer that contains the graphic you want to export. Be sure to turn off the eye icons from the layers you don't want to export.*

This method is very useful if you are using Photoshop as a web page layout tool, as described in Chapter 11, *Laying Out Pages in Photoshop.* You can keep your file intact and convert individual layers containing specific graphics one at a time into the GIF89a format. It's also convenient for creating GIF animations, since you can create your entire animation in one Photoshop file and export each layer out as a separate GIF file.

Using this layer method, you'll still have to go through several steps to create a graphic that contains a transparent area. And you'll have to rely on the merely sufficient indexing tools in the GIF89a Export module.

To use layers to create transparent GIFs, follow these steps:

1. Organize all the graphics for your web page in layers. (See Figure 5-14.)

2. Target and select the layer or layers containing the image you want to export. Turn off the eye icons for all the other layers. If you keep other eye icons on, you'll export more layers than you want.

3. Crop the file to the size you want to export, so the final GIF won't contain large blank areas.

4. Choose the GIF89a Export module; notice how the GIF89a dialog shown in Figure 5-15 differs from the dialogs we've seen earlier. This is because our graphic is still in the RGB mode, and needs to be indexed. With this dialog, you can choose how your RGB graphic is color indexed (with the Palette and Colors settings) and what color will be used as the background color (Transparency Index Color). You can also choose Load for custom color palettes, such as the browser-safe palette. Keep in mind that even with all these options, the GIF89a Export module doesn't give you as much control over the indexing process as you would have if you went directly from RGB to Indexed Color mode in Photoshop. However, if you want to use the layer method described here, you have no choice but to use the GIF89a Export module's indexing options.

5. Click Preview after you've chosen your color indexing options. The Preview dialog appears, as shown in Figure 5-16. The color swatch at the bottom shows exactly what and how many colors are contained in the graphic. You cannot edit these colors. You can use the Hand tool to move the image around the frame and the Zoom tool to zoom in and out. Click OK to close the dialog.

6. You can reset the image to its original colors by pressing Option/ Alt and clicking Reset. Once you're satisfied with the results, click OK, name, and save your GIF file.

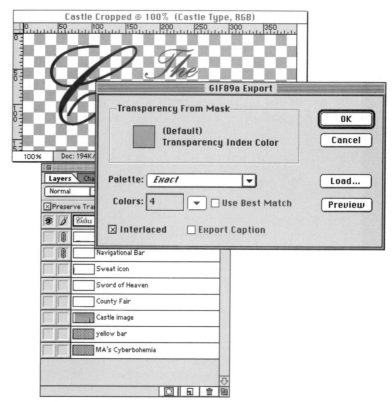

Figure 5-15. *When you export a layer from Photoshop to the GIF89a Export module, you get this dialog box*

When you export a Photoshop layer to the GIF89a Export module, you will achieve a transparent effect only if your layer is transparent.

How can you tell if you are working with a transparent layer? Easy: a checkered pattern is visible (or whatever pattern you've set your transparency settings to in Preferences). If no checks are visible, you've either inadvertently left on additional layers or you are working with a background layer. Be sure all eye icons are off, except the one on the targeted layer.

Creating glow effects with the layer method

Using a transparent layer and the GIF89a Export module, it's easy to create a soft, dreamy effect that will add zing to your web page. To have your graphic actually appear to glow, follow these steps:

1. With any of the selection tools, select the portion of your graphic that you want to glow.

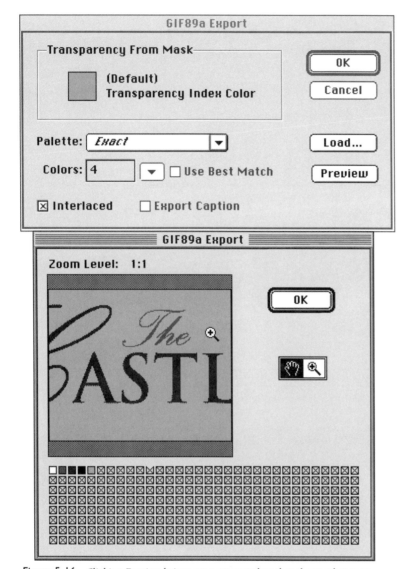

Figure 5-16. *Clicking Preview brings up a separate box that shows what your indexed image will look like*

2. Feather the selection (Select: Feather) at least 10 pixels, as shown in Figure 5-17.

3. Choose Select: Inverse and delete the selected area, as shown in Figure 5-18.

4. If you are working with a single-layer image, double-click the Background layer and rename it, so the layer can contain transparency. If you are working with an image containing multiple

layers, be sure to target the layer you are working on and turn off the eye icons of the other layers.

5. Open the GIF89a Export dialog. Notice the Transparency Index Color box—this is the secret to creating that cool look. It is set at default gray, but you can click on it to change it to any color with the color picker. Use the color picker to choose a color that matches the color of your web page background.

Figure 5-17. *To create a glow effect, start by feathering a selection at least 10 pixels*

Figure 5-18. *Cut your feathered, selected area to transparent*

Figure C-48 shows the results of setting the transparency index color to the same color as the web page background. Voila! It now has the soft, dreamy glow.

If you leave the transparency index color at the default gray, you won't like the results, shown in Figure C-49.

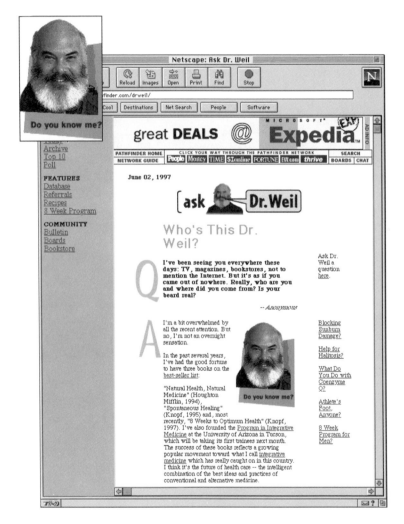

Figure 5-19. *The original GIF was created against a white background with no designated transparency. When placed on a web page with a white background, it appears to float on the page.*

A transparent look without transparent colors

You can create a transparent look without using the GIF89a Export module. Simply create your graphic on a sample of the background color or pattern. The background of your graphic will merge with the background of the page—making it appear to float in space— when you place it on a web page.

This method has its limitations. (Anything this simple must have a drawback, right?) Background colors often shift from platform to platform and from browser to browser. This means your image may be left high and dry on a viewer's monitor, its rectilinear edges evident against the web page background. And of course it won't work at all on patterned backgrounds.

HotWired designer Judd Vetrone used this technique effectively in Photoshop to simply cut and paste a photo onto a white background, the same color as his web page background (shown in Figure 5-19). He used the GIF file format because the image was small to begin with and he could be assured that there would be no color shift between the background color of the image and the background color of the page.

Familiarity counts

The ability to create transparent areas in your graphic is fundamental to good web design. In this chapter, we've shown you three basic ways to do this using Photoshop's GIF89a Export module. Regardless of which method you use—color selection, apply mask, or direct from a Photoshop layer—it pays to experiment and take the time to get familiar with the ins and outs of the module. Before long, you'll wonder how you ever did without it.

CHAPTER SIX

JPEG: ALL THE COLOR YOU WANT

N ow that you've seen that creating GIFs for the Web can be as tedious as rebuilding a car engine—from selecting a color palette, choosing the optimal color depth, and deciding whether or not to dither—you're in for a pleasant surprise. Creating JPEGs for the Web is the automotive equivalent of changing your engine oil.

In this chapter, you'll learn the effects of compression settings on image quality and file size. You'll learn how to prepare an image for compression to get the best of both worlds. You'll also learn how best to covert from color to black and white, and how to use JPEG plug-ins to get compression rates Photoshop can't touch.

Compression versus quality

To get a JPEG just right, you need to strike a fine balance between quality and file size. With Photoshop, you can choose how much compression is applied. If you apply too little compression, you'll have a beautiful image that's way too big for the Web.

When you save an image as a JPEG in Photoshop 4.0, you're presented with a dialog box to specify several settings, as shown in Figure 6-1. The most important of these is the compression slider, used for setting the level of compression. The slider is organized by image quality, so 10 (the highest quality) offers the least compression and 0 (the worst quality) offers the most compression. There's also a pop-up menu with four quality settings—low, medium, high, and maximum—which correspond to numeric values on the slider.

Earlier versions of Photoshop offered only 4 quality/compression settings, so having 11 settings in Photoshop 4.0 is a great improvement. Even so, the JPEG format offers more compression than Photoshop. The HVS JPEG and ProJPEG plug-ins, for instance, offer

In this chapter

- Compression versus quality
- Saving JPEG files
- Everything dithers
- Optimizing for compression
- Making better grayscale images
- Converting GIF to JPEG
- Premium JPEGs: a case study
- Pushing the envelope

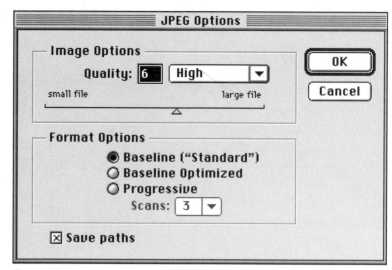

Figure 6-1. *The JPEG compression dialog box in Photoshop 4.0*

100 possible compression settings. See Appendix B, *Third-Party Software*, for more about these and other Photoshop plug-ins.

Because JPEG images can contain up to 16.8 million colors and still compress to a small file size, JPEG is best used on photographic images and graphics that contain subtle gradations in tone or color. Because it's a "lossy" technology—it literally throws away high-frequency data—JPEG is not good for line drawings, text, or any graphic than contains intricate detail. Unlike with the GIF89a file format, you cannot make part of a JPEG image transparent.

Let's look at some examples. First let's take a colorized photograph of a parrot. Figure C-50 shows the original Photoshop file. It weighs in at 116K. Figure C-51 shows the image as a JPEG saved with the highest quality setting. Figure C-52 shows the same image with Photoshop's lowest quality setting. As you can see, there's not an awful lot of image degradation, even at the maximum compression setting.

Table 6-1 shows the effect on image size.

Table 6-1. *File sizes and compression ratios achieved by Photoshop 4.0's JPEG compression settings for the parrot photo*

Compression Setting	File Size (in kilobytes)	Compression Ratio
10	55.3	2:1
9	36.4	3:1
8	26.3	5:1

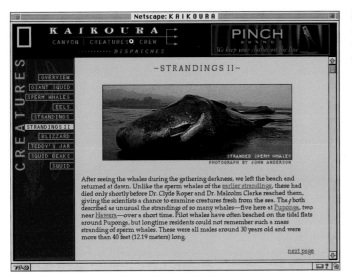

Figure C-1. *A properly processed photo sets a tone of professionalism that permeates an entire site, as does the one shown here in a page that Second Story designed for the National Geographic Society.*

Figure C-2. *Second Story's home page.*

Figure C-3. *As the histogram shows, poor distribution of tones results in too much contrast.*

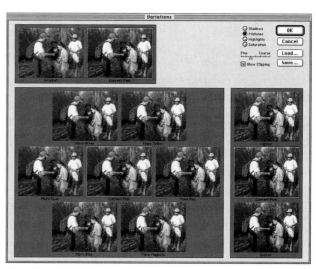

Figure C-5. *Variations will get you in the ballpark with color and contrast adjustment, but for more control, you'll need to use Photoshop's other correction tools.*

Figure C-4. *This photo contains an even distribution of tonal values, as shown by the histogram.*

Figure C-6. *The blue is gone—after a lot of work.*

Figure C-7. *Brad Johnson applied a Gaussian blur to a duplicate layer to improve this photograph taken with a digital camera. He also applied the tint method.*

Figure C-8. *Should this photographic image be a JPEG? That's what HotWired's Luke Knowland initially thought. But when he looked at a JPEG version on an 8-bit display system, he saw dithering that distracted from the image. Converting the image into a transparent GIF gave better results.*

Figure C-9. *Surely this Batman should be a JPEG. The image contains subtle variations in color that would be best represented with thousands of colors. But Knowland tried it as a GIF file (adaptive palette, diffusion dithering). The image dithers, of course, and that's what Knowland liked about it. The dithering actually enhanced the image by giving it a velvety texture.*

Figure C-10. *For this page, Knowland first saved the graphic as a GIF; however, at points of subtle color transition, the image broke up into distracting bands that looked like the rings of Saturn. Clearly 256 colors weren't enough to represent the graphic adequately. He chose JPEG instead, and it looks fine when it dithers on 8-bit monitors.*

Figure C-11. *Casey Caston is no fan of JPEG: he hates it. Sure, JPEG is great for creating a small file. But poorly applied JPEG compression gives weird color shifts and blocky patterns. He especially doesn't like the way JPEGs dither on an 8-bit monitor. For the mug shot on this c\net page, for example, Caston used a GIF for a photograph in order to maintain precise colors and sharp text.*

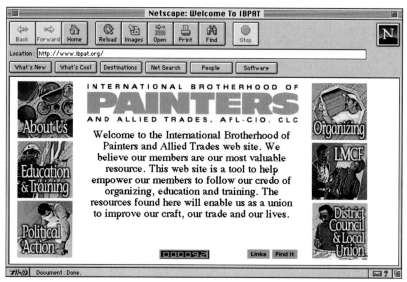

Figure C-12. *Option X's Sean Parker received several JPEG files with instructions to put them on the page as soon as possible. While converting to GIF would keep the text sharp, it would also mean reducing the colors and possibly changing the overall look and feel of the page. With time at a premium, he stayed with the JPEG format, knowing the result wouldn't be perfect. He managed to reduce the JPEGs to 3.5K each.*

Figure C-13. *As part of an experiment with JavaScript, Venu's Gregg Hartling created the page on the left using both JPEG and GIF images. The image on the right shows the individual elements and how they were put together. The woman's face was saved as a JPEG, as was the entire lower part of the page. The text blocks to the right and above her face were saved as GIFs. Breaking the page up like this takes advantage of the best properties of each format.*

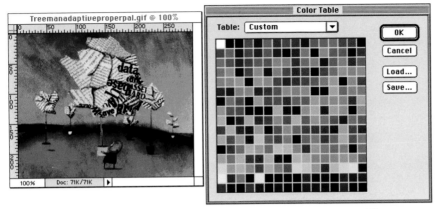

Figure C-14. *The color index defines which colors will be used in an image. (Illustration by James Yang.)*

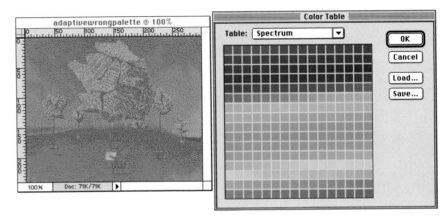

Figure C-15. *Changing the index changes the colors in the image.*

Figure C-16. *Best quality, large file size: 8-bit adaptive palette, 52K.*

Figure C-17. *Poor quality, small file size: 3-bit adaptive palette, 22K.*

Figure C-18. *Medium quality, medium file size: 5-bit adaptive palette, 31K.*

Figure C-19. *Good quality, medium file size: 6-bit adaptive palette, 36K.*

Figure C-20. *This image creates problems because it includes flesh tones and a multicolored background.*

Figure C-21. *When the standard adaptive palette is applied, the colored background throws off the flesh tones.*

Figure C-22. *Selecting the face before indexing tweaks the adaptive palette toward the flesh tones and away from the background colors.*

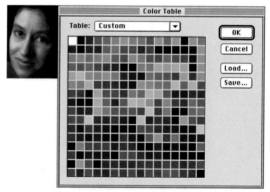

Figure C-23. *The cropped image and the resulting color table.*

Figure C-24. *The custom palette applied to the original image.*

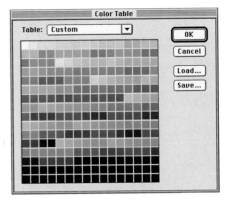

Figure C-25. *The browser-safe palette.*

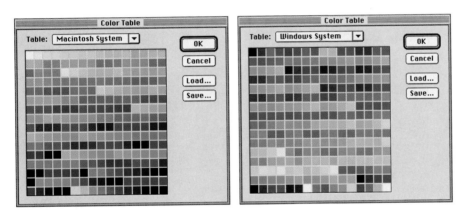

Figure C-26. *Macintosh and Windows system palettes.*

Figure C-27. *Web palette, no dither. At 7.7K, the egg looks crunchy, the smoke banded with rings of the wrong grays.*

Figure C-28. *Adaptive palette, diffusion dither. At 9.3K, the image looks fine, but the colors—the yellow background, the green text, and the red logo—have all shifted. Plus, it's the largest file so far.*

Figure C-29. *The combination approach. Coming in at 8.1K, the image was started in RGB mode. The egg and plane were copied to the clipboard. Then the image was indexed using the system palette with no dither. Casey then copied the still-in-RGB-mode egg/plane image from the clipboard into the indexed image. Once placed, the egg and plane automatically dither, while the rest of the image remains the same. This is the image that ran on c\net.*

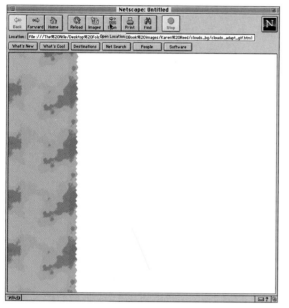

Figure C-30. *Non-browser-safe colors in background tiles don't dither, they shift.*

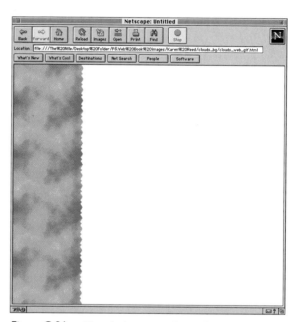

Figure C-31. *The solution is to index with the browser-safe palette.*

Figure C-32. *The dragon as it appeared on the GATE site.*

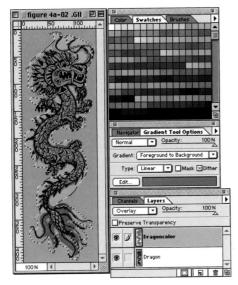

Figure C-33. *Corey Hitchcock used Photoshop's Gradient tool and browser-safe colors to create a dynamic web illustration.*

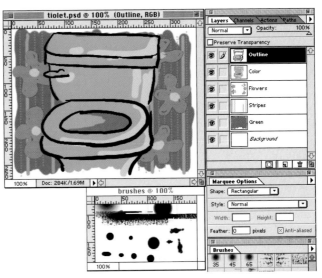

Figure C-34. *Brian Frick uses layers that contain each graphical element—easily accessible for later edits. Also notice the window titled "brushes," which he keeps handy so he can quickly create custom brushes that give him control over the colors used in his web illustrations.*

Figure C-35. *Designer Valerie Stambaugh created this self-portrait entirely in Photoshop's Indexed Color mode. Although this mode offers fewer options than RGB, it has the advantage of total predictability.*

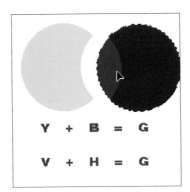

Figure C-36. *When seen this way, it looks as if there are three distinct colors.*

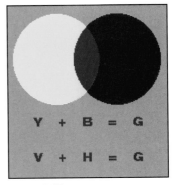

Figure C-37. *When the circles are joined, it now looks as if they are actually overlapping—an effect that is normally impossible in Photoshop's Indexed Color mode.*

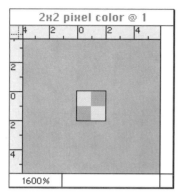

Figure C-38. *Creating a 2 x 2-pixel image and filling alternating pixels with similar browser-safe colors creates a hybrid color.*

Figure C-39. *These hybrid colors were created simply by filling a 2-pixel-wide horizontal selection with browser-safe colors.*

Figure C-40. *Hybrid colors can also be created by applying random noise to a selection and then applying Photoshop's Web palette.*

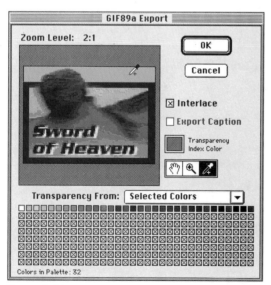

Figure C-41. *The Indexed Color version of the GIF89 Export dialog.*

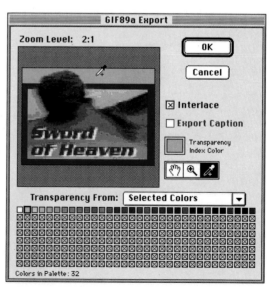

Figure C-42. *The selected color turns gray, indicating that it is transparent.*

Figure C-43. *Simply selecting the background color didn't work here, since part of the image also turned transparent.*

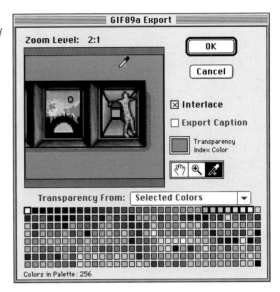

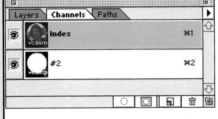

Figure C-44. *A new layer contains the "Webmo" text and background shape.*

Figure C-45. *Brian Frick created this illustration for Discovery Online by applying a mask to create transparent areas.*

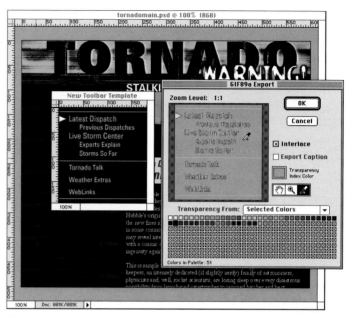

Figure C-46. *While selecting the background color as transparent appears to damage anti-aliased text, the effect works because the color from the web page fills in the missing pixels.*

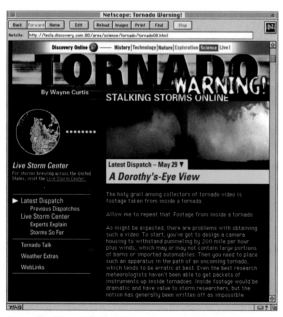

Figure C-47. *On the final web page, the type melds perfectly with the multicolored background. And there are no halos.*

Figure C-48. *This soft glow is only possible if you match the Transparency Index Color with the background color.*

Figure C-49. *This is what happens when we left the Transparency Index Color at its default gray rather than changing it to match the white background.*

Figure C-50. *The original RGB image.*

Figure C-51. *The same, saved as a JPEG at Photoshop's highest quality setting.*

Figure C-52. *Saved as a JPEG at Photoshop's lowest quality setting.*

Figure C-53. *Compressed at 90:1, the image falls apart into huge squares of color.*

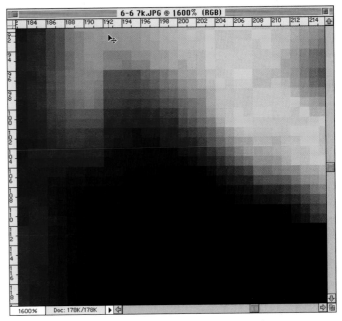

Figure C-54. *Magnification showing compression artifacts.*

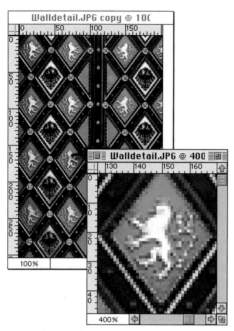

Figure C-55. *Saved at Photoshop 4.0's JPEG Low setting, this detailed, high-contrast photo falls apart, loses detail, and still takes up 24K.*

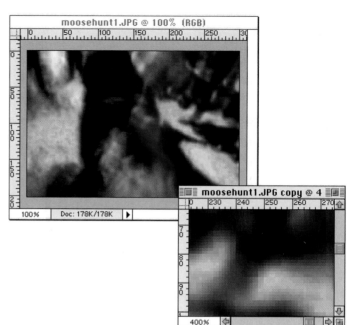

Figure C-56. *Also saved at Photoshop 4.0's JPEG Low setting, this impressionistic photograph falls apart from extreme compression, but the effect is not as noticeable because of the nature of the image. It takes up only 7K.*

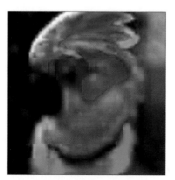

Figure C-57. *Progressive JPEGs load in passes, with each pass adding resolution and detail.*

Figure C-58. *JPEGs dither on 8-bit systems. End of story.*

Figure C-59. *With no optimizing, this JPEG image takes up a total of 50.3K.*

Figure C-60. *With selective blurring to the background sky, the JPEG image takes up 47K.*

Figure C-61. *With selective blurring to the background sky and global blurring, the JPEG image takes up 43K.*

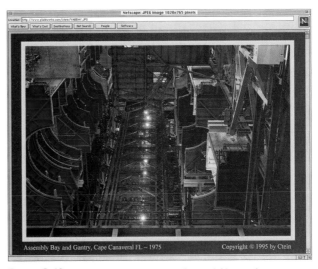

Figure C-62. *Although this 1020 x 765-pixel file weighs in at 497K, the quality is superlative, thanks to Gaussian blurring and careful image processing. It was converted to JPEG with a Photoshop 2.5 setting of 7.*

Figure C-63. *Here is Marc Andreessen in color.*

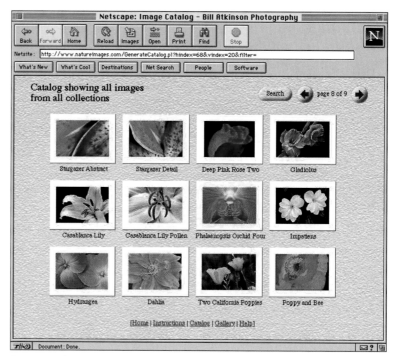

Figure C-64. *Here's a sampling of Bill Atkinson's 117 x 85-pixel thumbnails.*

Figure C-65. *Bill achieves a higher quality version by resizing down, as shown in this 320 x 480-pixel image.*

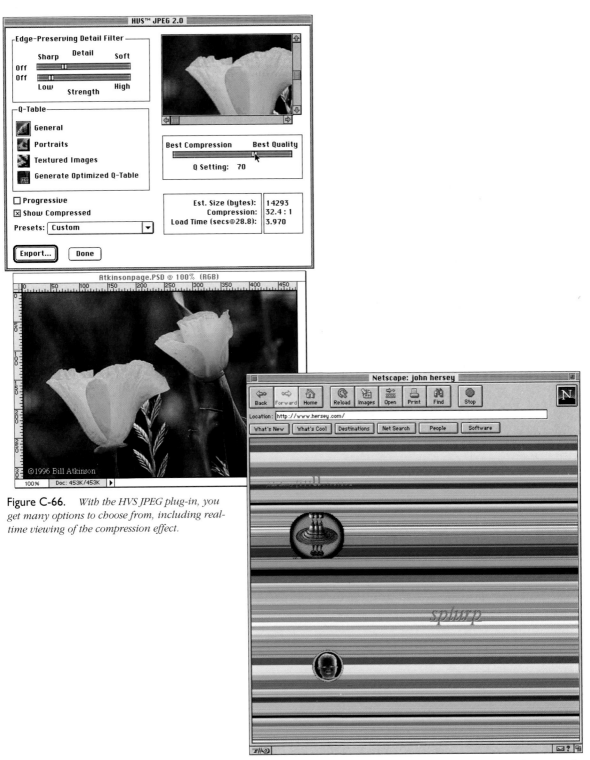

Figure C-66. *With the HVS JPEG plug-in, you get many options to choose from, including real-time viewing of the compression effect.*

Figure C-67. *John Hersey created this web page with color from a single 2 x 367-pixel color strip saved as a JPEG.*

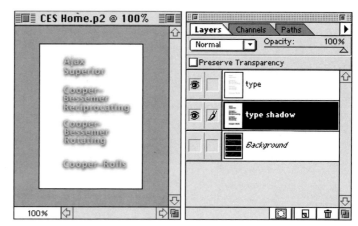

Figure C-68. *Applying a slight Gaussian blur behind type makes it more readable against a background.*

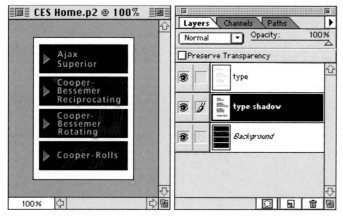

Figure C-69. *Without the Gaussian blur, the text is softer and harder to read.*

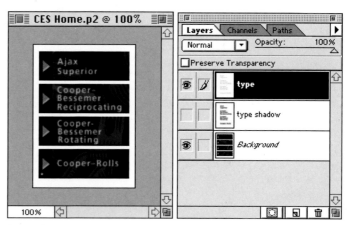

Figure C-70. *With a slight Gaussian blur, the yellow type pops out from the blue-green background.*

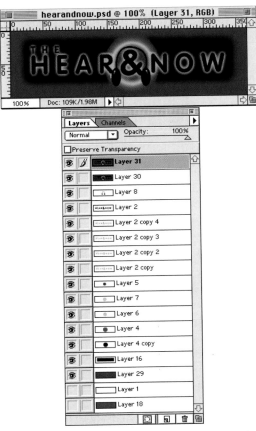

Figure C-71. *Corey Hitchcock created this neon look in just a few easy steps.*

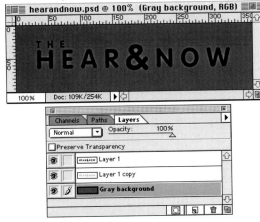

Figure C-72. *Next, fill the duplicated type with yellow, and apply a Gaussian blur.*

Figure C-73. *As each layer containing yellow type is turned on, the intensity of the color grows, until you have a neon-like effect.*

Figure C-74. *This type has been filled with the parrot image.*

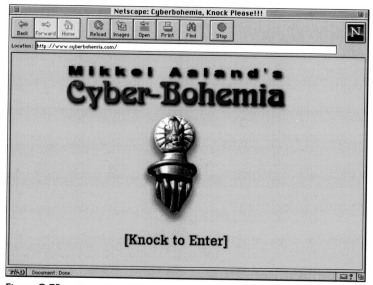

Figure C-75. *The "Cyber-Bohemia" type was created with clipping paths used as layer masks.*

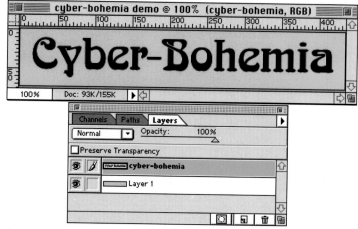

Figure C-76. *Here's the "Cyber-Bohemia" type brought into Photoshop and placed on its own layer.*

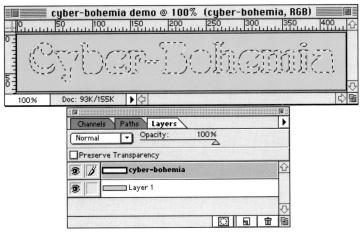

Figure C-77. *Delete the black fill before applying the Gradient tool.*

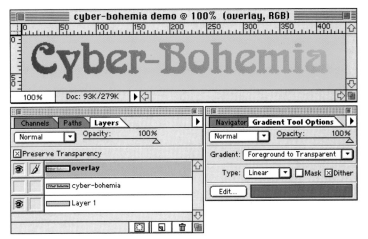

Figure C-78. *Use the Gradient tool with caution. It introduces non-browser-safe colors.*

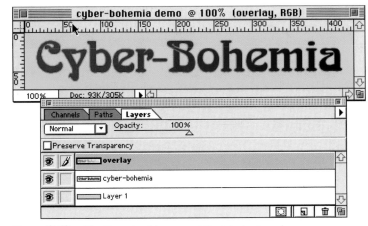

Figure C-79. *The Gaussian blur caused the type to spread.*

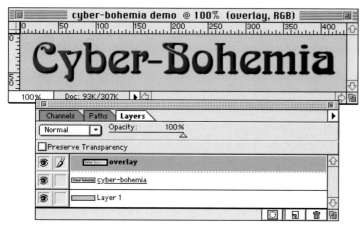

Figure C-80. *Applying the clipping path constrains the blurred type to its original shape.*

Figure C-81. *Stroking and textures added zing to the display type on this page.*

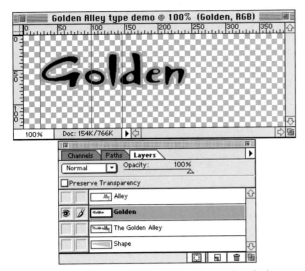

Figure C-82. *The "Golden" type is selected and stroked.*

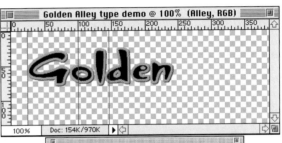

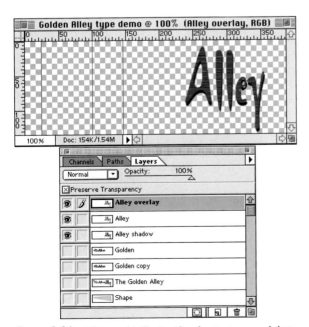

Figure C-84. *The word "Alley" with color, texture, and drop shadow applied.*

Figure C-83. *To create a drop shadow, the type is duplicated on a new layer, filled with a color, and offset from the original.*

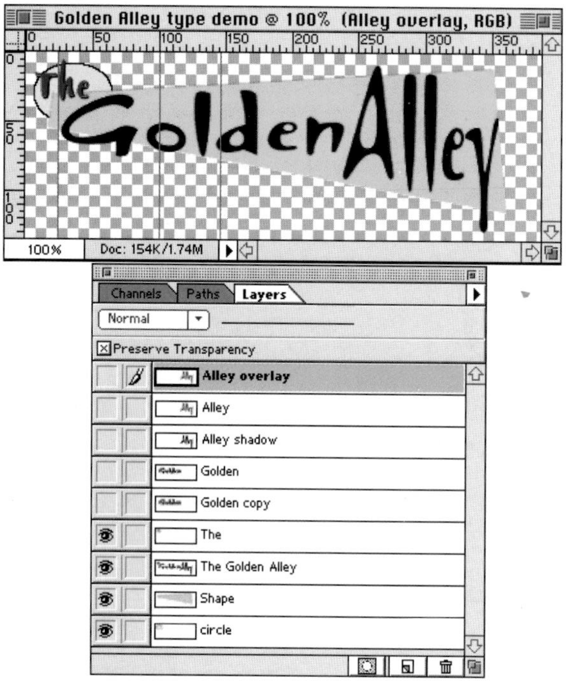

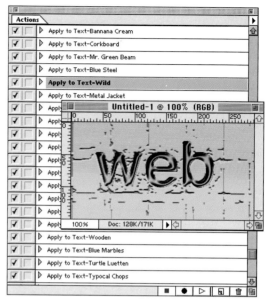

Figure C-85. *A blue oval is placed beneath the drop-shadowed word "The."*

Figure C-86. *An exotic type effect created with one of the actions from the KPT Actions Accessory Kit.*

Figure C-87. *With an 8-bit mask, PNG images blend seamlessly with the background.*

Figure C-88. *PNG offers a realistic, colored shadow effect.*

Table 6-1. *File sizes and compression ratios achieved by Photoshop 4.0's JPEG compression settings for the parrot photo (continued)*

Compression Setting	File Size (in kilobytes)	Compression Ratio
7	20.4	6:1
6	16.7	7:1
5	13.3	9:1
4	13.2	9:1
3	11.1	10:1
2	9.8	12:1
1	8.7	13:1
0	7.2	17:1

While you might suppose that each step reduced file size by a standard amount, you can see from this chart that this is not the case, at least for this image. (Remember that every image is different and the effects of JPEG compression will vary depending on the characteristics of your image.)

Notice, for instance, that the image compressed at 10 is half the original (2:1) and the image compressed at 9 is a third of the original's file size (3:1). But compressing the file at 8 yields a file that is one-fifth the size of the original. Thus, there's a huge bonus for compressing at 8 instead of 9. Further down the chart, you'll see that levels 5 and 4 both compress at 9:1, with a difference of just 200 bytes. Finally there's a dramatic increase in compression when going from 1 to 0.

Amazingly, even at 17:1 compression, the parrot image holds up pretty well. But as mentioned above, Photoshop's 0 setting isn't really maximum JPEG compression. Photoshop plug-in HVS JPEG offers much more extreme compression than this. Admittedly, you may not want to push compression much further than Photoshop's maximum compression setting, but it's handy to be able to compress heavily when you want to. And with 100 possible compression steps, various plug-ins offer a greater ability to fine-tune your image than Photoshop does.

So what does an over-compressed image look like? Figure C-53 is a fair example. This image has been compressed at HVS JPEG's 6 setting, which yields a 1.3K file, for a 90:1 compression rate.

Obviously this image is unacceptable. The image has broken down into blocks of color. There are hard lines around each block and very poor color transitions between adjacent blocks.

What's happening here? This image actually provides a good view into the behavior of the JPEG compression algorithm. When you save a file as a JPEG, the algorithm samples the image in 8 × 8 squares—one at a time. It's looking for similarities in tone and contrast. It then transforms each block into mathematical equations that represent the relevant color and brightness values. Saving data this way is much more efficient than saving the RGB values of each pixel, but the process discards RGB data that is deemed less important.

At lower compression rates, we usually don't notice that data is missing, because JPEG takes advantage of the psycho-physics of human perception and throws away the spatial frequencies (mostly the higher ones) that the human eye is least likely to notice. At higher compression rates, more and more data is thrown away, until the image breaks down.

To understand high and low spatial frequency, think of a bearded man's face: the thousands of fine strands of hair that make up the beard are considered high spatial frequency, while the smooth, relatively consistent areas of exposed skin are of low spatial frequency.

If you magnify a highly compressed JPEG image, you can actually see distinct blocks of pixels that are the artifacts of this sampling process, as shown in Figure C-54. The more compression that has been applied, the more evident these squares are.

As we saw above, the parrot photograph, with its subtle gradations and generally soft characteristics, compressed quite well, even at 17:1. Generally, softer or more impressionistic images maintain quality at higher compression rates, while very detailed images do not. Also, images with lower contrast compress more, with less degradation, than images with higher contrast, as shown in Figures C-55 and C-56.

Saving JPEG files

Now that you have a better understanding of what happens in JPEG compression, let's look at the process of saving JPEG files in Photoshop.

When you're ready to save your file as a JPEG, simply select Save or Save As, change the file format to JPEG, give your file a name with the extension .jpg or .jpeg, and click OK. (Note that if you have multiple layers, you'll have to flatten the layer before the Save As dialog will let you save it as anything but a Photoshop file. The Save A Copy dialog, however, automatically flattens the image when you choose the JPEG format.)

Next, you'll see the JPEG Options dialog, shown earlier in Figure 6-1, which contains the compression slider, as well as a choice of format options, and an option to "Save paths."

JPEG format options

There are three format options for JPEG files:

Baseline (Standard)

> This is the default setting, since it is universally supported.

Baseline (Optimized)

> This is a new option in Photoshop 4.0, and represents an evolution in the JPEG standard. When you choose this option, you get an image slightly smaller in file size (a couple hundred bytes) with better color fidelity. Current web browsers support this format. There are, however, other (mostly older) programs that have trouble opening a baseline-optimized JPEG. If you have any doubts about what program will be used to open your image, you should choose the Baseline (Standard) option.

Progressive

> These JPEGs are useful for large files that take a long time to download. If you choose this option, your image will be displayed in a series of passes; the image improves in quality with each pass.

Baseline JPEGs, whether standard or optimized, are stored as a single top-to-bottom scan of the image. The progressive format contains the same data and is about the same file size, but the data is displayed in a series of scans. The first scan appears quickly because it is equivalent to a low-quality setting, as shown in Figure C-57. With each subsequent scan, more data is provided. Progressive JPEG files are slightly smaller than baseline-standard files.

When you choose Progressive, you can choose the number of scans it takes for the entire image to appear (3, 4, or 5 scans). The actual speed of each scan depends on the transmission speed of the user's system and the computer that receives and decompresses the data. With a very fast computer hooked up to an ISDN line, the image appears nearly instantly, no matter how many scans you choose. Increasing the number of scans increases the file size very slightly—the difference is no more than 200 bytes or so.

While the current browsers support progressive JPEGs, some older browsers don't, so you may not want to want to use the progressive format on your primary pages.

Apples and oranges

While the quality settings of different versions of Photoshop produce roughly the same results, they cannot be compared with the quality settings of Photoshop JPEG plug-ins or conversion programs. For example, a Photoshop *Low* is not the same as a Debabilizer *Low*. For the most part, however, default settings (*Medium* for Photoshop, *Baseline* for Debabelizer) usually produce similar results.

Previewing JPEGs

The first time you save a JPEG, you may be surprised to see that the compressed JPEG file looks just as good as your original Photoshop file. Actually, it doesn't. Unfortunately, Photoshop doesn't display the effects of JPEG compression upon saving. You'll need to close and then reopen the image file to see what your new file looks like. This is another area where the JPEG plug-ins are more efficient and powerful than Photoshop itself.

The process

Since your goal is to create the smallest possible file while maintaining acceptable image quality, I recommend you start with heavy compression and then back off. When you preview the compressed image, zoom in and look for loss of detail or for compression artifacts. If the image looks OK, you're home free. If not, note the file size and try compressing the original at a higher quality setting. Keep backing off until you reach a good compromise between file size and quality.

Sometimes, depending on the image, you can produce very good quality at Photoshop's lowest setting. Even the 0 setting can be used on some images. Most often you'll settle on Photoshop's medium settings (3–5), which is a good compromise between quality and file size.

Remember that every time you open, manipulate, and save an image in the JPEG format, you lose data. Not only do you lose data, you increase the risk of creating a larger file size. Those distinct blocks of pixels that you saw earlier, the ones that resulted from applying high JPEG compression to an image, actually add high spatial frequency to the image. The more high spatial frequency information in an image, the less efficient the JPEG compression. It's always best to save your original in the Photoshop format (or other 24-bit format) and save subsequent JPEG files from the original.

Another point to remember is that you always lose some data when you compress with JPEG. If you want your image viewed at its best—if you are a visual artist, for example, presenting your portfolio for art directors to view and evaluate—you'll probably settle for only the highest quality settings (9–10). Keep in mind that even when you choose Maximum, there is some loss of image quality that can never be replaced. JPEG compression is never lossless; some image data is always lost.

As discussed earlier, JPEG is not a very good format for text and lines. If you must use JPEG on images with sharp-colored edges, such as text, you'll get better results if you choose the Maximum setting. This is because at this setting Photoshop automatically turns off *Chroma downsampling*, a process that works well with photographic images but causes fuzziness or jaggedness around the edges of hard lines. Chroma downsampling samples color areas at a rate of 2×2 pixels rather than 1×1 pixel. This relatively coarse method of throwing away color data results in smaller file sizes but creates 2 pixel jaggies around sharp color boundaries.

Automating the process

If you have a lot of images, there's no doubt about it—cycling through all the JPEG settings for every image is a real pain. Why not set up an Action to save your file at different compression settings, so you can easily compare and decide which setting you want? That's what Sean Parker of Option X did. His JPEG comparison Action is shown in Figure 6-2. His Action, which you can easily duplicate, makes it quick and easy to compare effects of different compression settings in Photoshop.

To create such an Action, simply record the process of saving a file in the JPEG format at different compression settings. Save this Action as your JPEG Action and apply it when needed.

Troubleshooting

If you're having trouble saving your file as a JPEG, make sure you've taken care of the following details:

- When you save an image in Photoshop, JPEG is an option only if your image is in the RGB (or CMYK) mode.

- All layers must be flattened before the JPEG option is available.

- Also note that if you have set your preferences to append the file suffix, Photoshop adds .JPG to your file name. Many servers don't accept capital letters, so it's a good idea to retype the appended letters in lowercase.

- Be sure to turn off the thumbnail options to keep the file size as small as possible.

Everything dithers

When you work with JPEG images, set aside what you've learned about browser-safe colors. There's no such thing as a browser-safe JPEG. JPEGs don't contain color lookup tables like GIFs. They save color data as an approximation of the original color. Figure C-58 shows a background created with browser-safe colors, then saved as

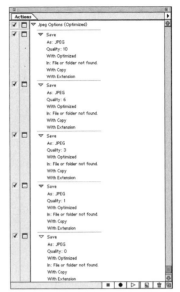

Figure 6-2. *Action for saving several versions of a file at different JPEG settings*

Checking the code

Although .jpg is the universally accepted file suffix for JPEG files, you'll never see the acronyms JPG or JPEG if you view the actual code of a JPEG file. That's because JPEG refers only to a family of compression algorithms, not to a specific file format. Instead, what you'll likely see is the acronym JFIF, which stands for JPEG File Interchange Format.

a JPEG and viewed on an 8-bit display system. The background
dithers, as will any JPEG image viewed on an 8-bit display system.

Also forget about matching the background of your image to the
background of your web page, the way you can do with GIF files.
On some 24-bit systems, you might get a match. But most of the
time you will be disappointed at the results. Remember, JPEG and
GIF colors rarely match, as shown in Figure 6-3. Even what you
think is pure white will dither, as shown in Figure 6-4.

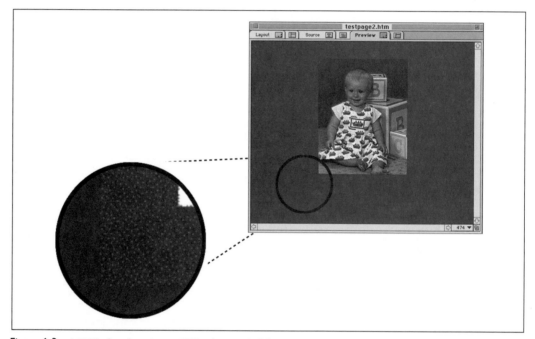

Figure 6-3. *A JPEG placed against a GIF background of the "same" color rarely matches on an 8-bit display*

Always keep in mind that while dithering is very distracting when it
appears on solid, flat colors, it can be a godsend on images with
smooth color transitions. If how your images look on lower-end
systems is important, you should preview the effect of dithering by
adjusting your system to 8-bit display or viewing your work on
someone else's system before compression.

Optimizing for compression

As we have shown, JPEG works best on images that contain smooth
transitions between colors and details. You can use this knowledge
to actually optimize an image so it compresses better with less loss
of quality.

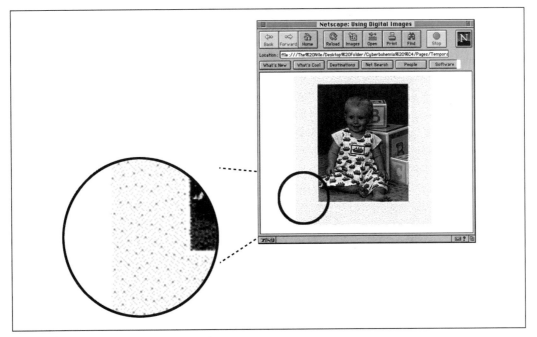

Figure 6-4. *Even white dithers in the JPEG format*

Selective blurring

Let's start by selectively applying a Gaussian blur before applying JPEG compression. This method can be applied to any image that has large expanses where detail is not critical. It is a method popular with web designers who are willing to spend a little extra time to get both small file size and high quality.

Figure C-59 shows an image with a large expanse of background area (sky and clouds) and details in the foreground (foliage and cityscape). The original Photoshop file is 300 × 440 pixels and is 398K. Saved with Photoshop's *Low* setting, with no optimizing, the file is 50.3K.

By blurring the selected background (with the Gaussian Blur filter set to .6) before JPEG compression, the file size is reduced to 47K, a 6% file size savings, with no loss of important details (see Figure C-60).

To push the benefits of blurring a little further, you can apply a Gaussian blur of .2 to the entire landscape—in addition to the .6 Gaussian blur applied to the sky. This results in a total savings of 14%. The resulting image is shown in Figure C-61.

Global blurring

Making images look good on the Web is a matter not only of aesthetics but also of commerce, for photographer, writer, and fine-print master, Ctein. Not represented by any gallery, he uses the Web to sell his work.

Ctein (that's his whole name) tweaks his electronic files to maximize quality, and the results are impressive. Figure C-62 shows a sampling of Ctein's web work. Working with a precisely calibrated monitor and Photoshop 2.5, he carefully adjusts the color and tonal balance of his scanned images, comparing the results with the original print. Then he applies a Gaussian blur to the entire image. He uses a blur radius of only .2 pixels, which does not produce any visible degradation of the image but results in JPEG files that are about 15% smaller than files of comparable quality. Even slight blurring, it turns out, will suppress some of the higher spatial frequencies enough to significantly reduce the JPEG file.

When Ctein uses Photoshop to convert his files to the JPEG file format, he usually uses a JPEG setting of 5, which results in a compression ratio of approximately 10:1. (This ratio will vary depending on the content of the image.) For some images he applies a setting of 6 or even 7. He is always looking for a compression setting that produces few or no artifacts larger than a single pixel in size.

All his images are placed against a neutral gray background that includes a grayscale swatch, so the viewer can calibrate his or her own monitor to the correct gamma, if desired, for the best viewing of Ctein's work. Ctein also includes a Macbeth Color chart on his site as a general calibration tool. (The Macbeth color chart is a standardized "test pattern" of colors such as pure red, green, and blue and tones such as white, black, and various shades of neutral gray. It is commonly used by photographers and graphic artists to maintain consistent color and tone throughout a variety of viewing situations.)

Ctein has sold many of his prints directly to web viewers. As testimony to his careful work, only one person has returned a print saying it's not what they expected. You can find his site at *www.plaidworks.com/ctein.*

Blurring in Lab mode

Photographer (and HyperCard inventor) Bill Atkinson suggests another way to optimize an image before applying JPEG compression. Like Ctein's method described previously, Bill's technique also involves using Gaussian Blur to suppress higher spatial frequencies.

However, if you convert your image from RGB to Lab color and then apply a Gaussian Blur to the *a* and *b* channels, you can actually apply much more blur and suppress more of the higher frequencies without noticeable effects. The *a* and *b* channels are pure color channels, so because of the nature of human vision, blurring isn't as noticeable.

The actual Gaussian blur setting you use will depend on the size of your image. I suggest you start with a setting of .5 pixels, then keep increasing the amount of blur until you overdo it. Then back off to a lower setting. After you convert back to RGB, apply JPEG compression. The larger your image, the more savings you'll get.

I tried Bill's method on the parrot image, ending up with a Gaussian blur setting of 5.0 with no noticeable degradation in image quality. At that setting, I shaved off 3K using Photoshop's High JPEG setting for a savings of about 10%, and I shaved off 2K from the Low JPEG setting for a 15% file size saving.

Making better grayscale images

Black and white images are often used on the Web, not only because they make smaller files, but also they stand out and grab attention in a gaudy, color-saturated world.

JPEG can compress grayscale images by a factor of about 5:1. This ratio is lower than the ratio for color images because JPEG compresses color data more effectively than brightness or grayscale data. However, because grayscale images are only 8 bits instead of 24 bits, you still end up with a significantly smaller file than if you had used a color image.

In Photoshop, when most users want to convert a color RGB image into grayscale, they simply choose Mode: Grayscale and leave the work up to Photoshop. But simply changing modes doesn't produce the best results.

You'll get better looking black and white images if you go through Photoshop's Lab color space because you can isolate the important brightness characteristics of an image rather than its superfluous (in the case of black-and-white images) RGB values.

To convert your color images into grayscale:

1. Convert your RGB image into the Lab color space (Image: Mode: Lab Color). Flatten the layers.

2. Go to the Channels palette and select the Lightness channel. Your image now appears in grayscale.

Figure 6-5. *Simply changing modes yields an image with blocked shadows*

Figure 6-6. *Using Lab mode creates a much better grayscale image—notice how smooth his skin looks in comparison to Figure 6-5*

3. Select channels *a* and *b* and delete them. Now you have isolated the grayscale data and discarded the color data.

4. Save your image as a Photoshop file. If you check the mode under Image: Mode, you'll see the image is in multichannel mode.

5. Convert to grayscale mode (Image: Mode: Grayscale).

6. Now you can edit the image as you wish—by changing the levels, for instance.

7. Save your file as a JPEG. In order to do this, you will need to convert back to the RGB mode. It will still appear as a grayscale image, but now you can save it as a JPEG at any compression ratio you wish.

Does this really make a difference? Consider a portrait I recently took of Netscape cofounder Marc Andreessen. Figure C-63 shows the original color photo. Figure 6-5 shows the results of simply converting from RGB to grayscale mode. Note the blocking in the shadows and the "chunky" look to the skin. Figure 6-6 shows the results of the Lab process. The midtones are smoother and the shadows are less murky.

Converting GIF to JPEG

What do you do if someone hands you an image that has been saved in the GIF format and you decide to incorporate it into another image that is best saved as a JPEG?

Generally it is not a good idea to use JPEG compression on images that have been color-indexed—especially photographic images. In the process of reducing and indexing colors, the image often becomes choppy or coarse. This is because there are fewer colors available to create smooth transitions. Dithering, while fooling the eye into believing that there are more colors, actually introduces even more noise at a sub-pixel level.

JPEG doesn't handle this high-spatial frequency noise well. The result is often a larger file size than you started with, as well as a lousy-looking image. Figure 6-7, for example, shows a menubar saved as a GIF and as a JPEG. The GIF (on top) was indexed using the browser palette and is 8.5K. The JPEG (on the bottom) is nearly twice the size, 15.1K. Although we used Photoshop's High JPEG setting, the image quality still isn't as good as the original GIF.

If you must turn an indexed file such as a GIF into a JPEG , first convert your file to RGB (or Lab color mode—see the previous section "Blurring in Lab mode"), then apply a Gaussian Blur to

Figure 6-7. *Images starting out as a GIF (top) and then converted to a JPEG (bottom) give less than desirable results*

soften the image as much as possible without noticeable visual degradation. When JPEG compression is applied, there will be less noise to interfere with the compression process.

Premium JPEGs: a case study

Bill Atkinson is a legend in the computer industry. Not only was he on the Apple computer team that created the Macintosh, he is the programmer who wrote the original QuickDraw program as well as MacPaint and HyperCard. Now he is retired and devotes his time to his passion, photography.

Along with his wife, graphic designer Sioux Atkinson, and fellow Apple legend Andy Herzfeld, Bill set up a web site to display and sell original prints of his photographic work, *www.natureimages.com*, shown in Figure C-64.

Bill achieves a beautiful effect on his web site through careful image processing and the use of a Photoshop plug-in called HVS JPEG, a product available from Digital Frontiers. Bill tried Photoshop's JPEG file converter, but found he could get better quality and compression using Digital Frontiers' product.

Here, step-by-step, from resizing to processing to finally applying HVS JPEG, is how Bill arrives at the quality that is so evident in his work:

1. *Resize in increments.* Bill starts by resizing his original digital file, which is typically 100–425 megabytes and saved in the Lab color mode. (His original files are so huge because they are scanned to create high-resolution Evercolor prints. These prints are made on a digital enlarger and then sold.)

He resizes one increment at a time, not all at once:

— First, he cuts his original file size in half.

— Then he applies Photoshop's Unsharp Mask filter. His settings for the filter are: Amount: 150%, Radius: 1.0, and Threshold: 0.

— Then he resizes this file in half and applies Unsharp Mask again with the same setting. This goes on until he reaches a file size of either 320 pixels tall for horizontal images or 320 wide for vertical images, as shown in Figure C-65.

By resizing in this manner, he is able to preserve more of the detail present in the original high-resolution scan. The process sounds tedious, but Bill has created a Photoshop 4.0 Action that does the entire job for him automatically, even applying the Unsharp Mask.

2. *Convert to RGB.* He then changes the mode from Lab to RGB and saves a copy of the file by adding the words "web size" to the filename. This file becomes a master file from which he creates both a Macintosh version and a PC version as well as thumbnails for both platforms.

3. *Create custom curves for different platforms.* He creates these different versions by applying a custom Photoshop curve (Image: Adjust: Curves). He arrived at the settings for the curves after visually analyzing the effect different monitors had on his images. One Curve adjusts his image to look good at a gamma of 1.8 (Macintosh) and another Curve makes his image look good at a gamma of 2.2 (PC). The custom Curves affect only the midtones of the image, not the color.

4. *Create thumbnails with Unsharp Mask.* To create the thumbnail version of each photograph, Bill resizes the full-size image in one-step increments until he has a horizontal image with a height of 64 pixels or a vertical image with a width of 64 pixels. After the first incremental resizing, he applies an Unsharp Mask filter with the following settings: Amount: 150%, Radius: .8, and Threshold: 0.

After the second incremental resizing step, he applies an Unsharp Mask once more (Amount: 100%, Radius: .6, and Threshold: 0). Again, he uses a Photoshop Action to carry out all these steps. He then increases the canvas size to 116 × 84 pixels (Image: Canvas Size), adds a white border, and then, for the final step, he adds a 1-pixel gray edge to the bottom and right edges to simulate a drop-shadow.

5. *Compress with HVS JPEG filter.* Finally, he manually applies JPEG compression to each image using the HVS JPEG filter, as shown in Figure C-66. First he moves the slider until he sees the image that is displayed in the HVS JPEG window break up or look particularly crusty. Then he pulls the slider back, applying less compression until the photograph appears to look right. HVS JPEG not only previews the effects of compression in real time, but also gives an approximation of the file size and the approximate download time based on a 28.8 modem. Bill also fine-tunes each image by experimenting with different HVS JPEG parameters. Most of the time, he sets his parameter to Textured Images. HVS JPEG actually pre-filters each image and determines what can and cannot be done to optimize an image for JPEG compression.

In Bill's (and wife Sioux's) web design, the photographs are placed on a gray background, with colorless navigational devices—leaving the color within the photograph to dominate the page. This way the energy is focused on the image, not elsewhere.

By the way, when you try this method, be sure to work on a copy of your original. Going from one color mode to another throws away data and may result in a degradation of quality.

Pushing the envelope

We started this chapter by saying how easy it is to create a JPEG. However, like so many things in life, if you want to push the envelope and get the most out of the format, you need to work at it. This means familiarizing yourself with the way JPEG works on different types of images, and taking the time to optimize your images *before* applying JPEG compression. If you do this, not only will the quality of your image improve, but you'll also save anywhere from 5 to 20% of your file size.

CHAPTER SEVEN

CREATING BACKGROUND TILES

Y ou can create an infinite number of custom backgrounds with Photoshop. If you use one of the methods described in this chapter and pay attention to file size, your background will download quickly and give your web site sizzle and pop.

Backgrounds have been a part of the Web for some time, and are now considered part of the HTML standard. To add a background to your page, simply add the BACKGROUND extension to your BODY tag. For example, the tag <BODY BACKGROUND="background.gif"> tiles the file *background.gif* across and down the browser window. The text and graphics in your page are displayed on top of the tiled background.

This method of creating a background is not as fast as using hexadecimal code to designate a single color, but if you make your tile small enough and pay attention to its total file size through color indexing and compression, your background will start to appear nearly instantly. (To specify a single color, use the following code: <BODY BGCOLOR="#FFFFFF">, where FFFFFF is the hexadecimal code for your color.)

You can use either GIF or JPEG files for backgrounds. If you use GIF files, you should use browser-safe colors. If you use JPEGs (something you might do if your background graphic contains subtle gradations or more than 256 colors), you may encounter distracting blotchy effects.

Most web designers use one of three basic techniques for creating backgrounds in Photoshop. One popular method is to create horizontal or vertical strips and selectively fill them with color or graphics. When loaded as a background into a browser, these strips repeatedly tile across and down until the browser window is filled.

In this chapter

- Working with tiling strips
- Creating patterns with square tiles
- Compressing backgrounds with JPEG
- Grabbing backgrounds
- Remembering the balance

This technique is often used to block out a sidebar area of a page, as shown in Figure 7-1. This technique is described in detail in the next section, "Working with tiling strips."

Figure 7-1. *For The Gate's home page, designer Corey Hitchcock created a background that acts as a sidebar, highlighting navigational controls*

The second method is to create a square tile. If prepared properly, the square will tile and create a seamless background not unlike patterned wallpaper. The image has to be prepared so that the edges will meld seamlessly from tile to tile. Figure 7-2 shows a page that uses this square tile technique. The technique is described in detail in the section "Creating patterns with square tiles."

The third method is to load a full-sized image or graphic as a background. Although this method produces unique, picturesque

Figure 7-2. *The Presbyterian Healthcare System home page uses seamless tiles for the background*

backgrounds, it is practical only if you can reduce the file—through careful color indexing or compression—to a manageable size. Figure 7-3 shows a site that used a single full-size image as a background. This technique is discussed in the section "Compressing backgrounds with JPEG."

Working with tiling strips

If you want to precisely control color and graphic changes in your background, you should use the tiling strip technique. With this technique you can place vibrant graphics in one part of the page, while leaving another part clutter-free for easy reading of text and other content. In this section, we'll go through the following applications for tiling strips:

- Soft-edged sidebars
- Ribbon-shaped sidebars
- Film-strip sidebars
- Color-band effects

Figure 7-3. *The background for Encyclopaedia Britannica's Shakespeare and the Globe site is a full-size JPEG image, compressed to 16K*

Making soft-edged sidebars

To create the background used on The Gate's home page (Figure 7-1), designer Corey Hitchcock used the Gradient tool to create the background image shown in Figure 7-4. This image is 1,377 pixels wide and 8 pixels high.

To create this background, Corey followed these steps:

1. She created a new file, 1377 × 8 pixels, and filled it with teal (Red = 153, Green = 204, Blue = 204).

2. Working from the left edge of the image, she used the rectangle marquee tool to make a selection 100 pixels wide and filled it with black (Red = 0, Green = 0, Blue = 0).

Figure 7-4. *This horizontal strip tiles to create the background for The Gate's home page*

3. To create a transition from the black to the teal she made a 15-pixel-wide rectangular selection, starting from the right edge of the black area.

4. She selected the Gradient tool and set the foreground color to black and the background color to gray. In the Gradient Tool Options palette, she made the following settings:

   — Gradient: Foreground to Background

   — Type: Linear

   — Opacity: 100%

   — Dither: On

5. While holding the Shift key (to constrain the tool to a straight line), she dragged the cursor across the selection from left to right. This created a straight, linear gradation from black on the left to gray on the right.

6. She added another black area to her strip, starting 700 pixels from the left and continuing all the way to the right edge of the graphic, because she didn't want the teal to tile off into infinity. She created a soft-edged look for this right sidebar in the same way as she did for the left sidebar, with the Gradient tool. (You don't see the black sidebar on the right in the screenshot because it is offscreen. You can see it in the actual graphic in Figure 7-4.)

Testing the strip

Once you've made your strip, you can simply code up your HTML, check it in a browser, go back to Photoshop to edit the graphic, and then repeat the process until you're satisfied. Ultimately, you'll need to check your work in a browser (more than one, preferably), but while you're working in Photoshop, wouldn't it be nice to get an idea of what the page will look like without having to switch to HTML? Here's how to simulate a tiled background page from within Photoshop:

1. Select all of your background graphic.

2. Define your graphic as a pattern by choosing Edit: Define: Pattern.

3. Create a new file. You can make this screen any size you want, but make it large enough to at least approximate the size of your end users' monitors. Something in the neighborhood of 640× 480 is appropriate.

4. Select Edit: Fill to bring up the Fill dialog box and choose Pattern from the Use pull-down menu. This option tiles the defined pattern to fill the current window, just as a browser would, as shown in Figure 7-5.

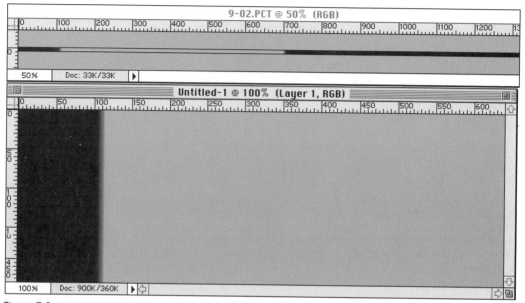

Figure 7-5. *To test background tiling, define your graphic as a pattern and fill a browser-sized file with that pattern. Photoshop will tile the graphic just like a browser*

Feathering for gradients

Corey used the Gradient tool to create a smooth transition from the sidebar color to the mainbar color. Here's another method for creating the same look by feathering a selection:

1. Create a 1000 × 8 pixel strip, either horizontal or vertical. Fill it with the color you want to use for the main area of the site (teal in The Gate example).

2. Make an *unfeathered* selection about 100 pixels from the edge. Fill the selection with the color for the sidebar area (black in The Gate example).

3. Open Select: Feather to bring up the Feather dialog box and choose a radius of 15 pixels or so.

4. Fill the feathered selection with the sidebar color you used in step 2. This creates a soft transition between the sidebar color and the main area color.

As shown in Figure 7-6, this makes a solid section of black, then a transitional area from black to teal, and finally the teal section.

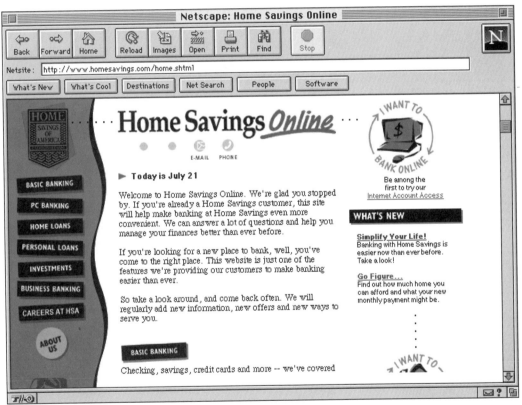

Figure 7-6. *The feathering technique creates a graduated look yet maintains a definite edge to the sidebar color*

Making ribbon-shaped sidebars

Of course, you're not stuck with rectangles for sidebar backgrounds. In Figure 7-7, the Home Savings of California's home page, designed by Venu Interactive, uses a ribbon-shaped sidebar, which is notable for the thin, elegant line of black to the right of the ribbon shape. The site uses different colored ribbons on different pages. This description focuses on the blue-green ribbon on the home page.

Figure 7-7. *Gregg Hartling of Venu Interactive created this ribbon-shaped sidebar for Home Savings of California*

Designer Gregg Hartling started the process by drawing a ribbon shape in Adobe Illustrator. Then he switched to Photoshop and followed these steps:

1. He created a new Photoshop file, 121 × 1200 pixels, created a new layer called *gray master,* and pasted the ribbon shape onto that layer.

2. He made several copies of this master layer, selected Preserve Transparency in the Layers palette, and filled each layer with a different color.

3. To make the black edge of the ribbon, he copied the master layer again, this time naming the new layer *black under-ribbon*. He selected the new layer and ran the Offset filter (Filters: Other: Offset) to offset the shape slightly up and to the right. Then he filled this version with black.

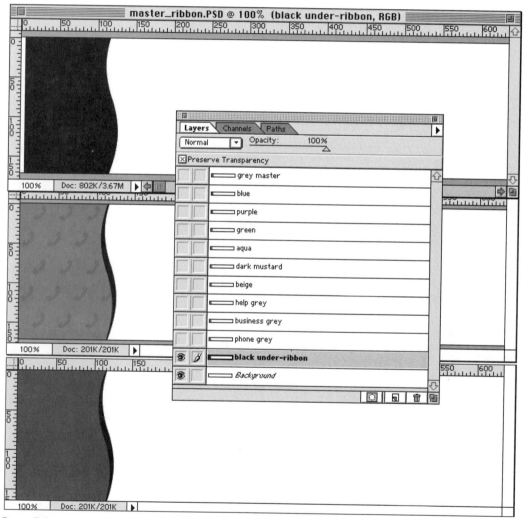

Figure 7-8. *The black under-ribbon layer (top) and several of the ribbons created as backgrounds*

4. He positioned the colored layer above the *black under-ribbon* layer, turned off the other layers, and saved out the various

versions of the ribbon background as GIF files. He ended up
with nine "different" backgrounds that he used throughout the
Home Savings site. The black under-ribbon and several variations are shown in Figure 7-8.

Working with bands of color

Figure C-67 shows the fanciful home page for illustrator John
Hersey. He created the background by making a 12-color bar in Illustrator, duplicating it several times, and then dragging and dropping
the file into Photoshop. Then he cropped the file to its final size of
2× 369 and saved it as a JPEG, shown in Figure 7-9. He chose JPEG
so he would be able to keep all the vibrant colors. It still looks fine
on monitors that display only 256 colors.

You can add your own colorful backgrounds by using Photoshop
4.0's Gradient Tool Options and Transparent Rainbow fill. To do this:

1. Create a vertical or horizontal strip. Select the Gradient tool.

2. From the Gradient Tool Options palette, select Transparent
   Rainbow from the Gradient pop-up menu, shown in Figure 7-10.
   (In Photoshop 4.0, you can edit the colors, transitions, and trans-
   parency settings by clicking on the palette's Edit button.)

3. Inside your horizontal or vertical strip, press the Shift key while
   dragging the cursor the entire length or width of your window
   to create a straight, even fill of color. When you release the
   cursor, a rainbow of colors will fill your background strip.

Figure 7-9. *The actual strip used to create the background in Figure C-67*

Be sure to test your work by using the fill-with-pattern method
explained earlier in the section "Making soft-edged sidebars." See
that your background doesn't overwhelm the rest of your page,
unless you want it to!

Figure 7-11 shows another background created as a strip that
combines both gradation and a graphical element. Created by Gregg
Hartling of Venu Interactive, the actual tile is 53 × 2600 pixels long,
so there isn't any chance that the black top area will repeat on a
viewer's monitor. The total file size is about 10K.

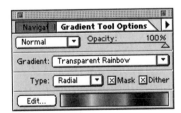

Figure 7-10. *Experiment with the settings in the Gradient Tool Options palette to create rainbow and other colored gradients*

Creating patterns with square tiles

You can create a repeating pattern while keeping your total file size
down by tiling squares. This technique is a bit trickier than using
tiling strips because all four edges of the square must blend or melt
into the adjacent square. If they don't match, you'll get the effect
shown in Figure 7-12. Sometimes this may work, but obviously it's

not a seamless pattern. The next section shows how to use Photoshop's Offset filter to make all four edges match.

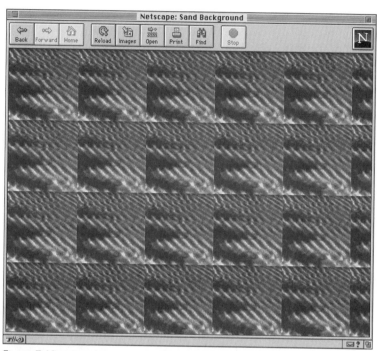

Figure 7-12. *If you just create a square tile and have the browser tile it across your page, you'll often wind up with "seams" between the tiles*

Creating seamless tiles with the Offset filter

When patterns are used discreetly, they work in harmony with the rest of the page, as in the home page for Presbyterian Healthcare System (shown in Figure 7-2) designed by Bea Garcia of Houston-based Savage Design. She drew the pattern in Illustrator and then brought it into Photoshop, where she created a browser-safe green background, touching up the leaves with a lighter green. To create seamless tiles, she cropped the image to 134 × 134 pixels and used the Offset filter, following these steps:

1.   She selected Filter: Other: Offset to bring up the Offset dialog box. In the Horizontal and Vertical boxes she entered values equal to half the dimensions of her image. Since her image was 134 pixels in each direction, she entered 67 in each box. This moves the image 67 pixels to the right and 67 pixels down, as shown in Figure 7-13.

Figure 7-11. *Venu's Gregg Hartling created this tiled background that combines a non-distracting graphic element with a slightly graduated header*

2. Then, in the Undefined Areas section of the Offset dialog box, she chose Wrap Around. This inverts the remaining portion of the image and tiles it in the unused areas (the part that was white in Figure 7-13). The former outer edges now meet in the center of the image (see Figure 7-14).

3. With the Rubber Stamp tool, she removed the seam caused by the outside edges meeting in the center and smoothed out the lines. The result is shown in Figure 7-15.

When she brought this image into the web page, the edges matched and she had a seamless background.

Connecting loose ends with the Offset filter

Here's an interesting problem. How do you get an intricate design—like the one Brian Frick created for a Discovery Online article on hackers, shown in Figure 7-16—to work as a tiled background? Surely it would be impossible to make all those little lines match up perfectly.

Once again, it's the Offset filter to the rescue. It's very difficult to give step-by-step instructions on this technique, but essentially, Brian drew the gadgets and wires with the pencil tool and periodically applied the Offset filter to connect the loose ends. He kept repeating the process until he got what he wanted. Figure 7-17 shows the image tile he came up with.

Figure 7-13. *Offsetting the image by half in each direction positions the top left corner of the image in the exact center of the window*

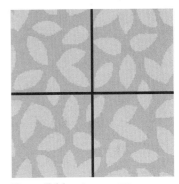

Figure 7-14. *Choosing Wrap Around tiles the remaining image around the center but leaves horizontal and vertical creases (increased here for emphasis)*

Figure 7-15. *The background tile with seams removed*

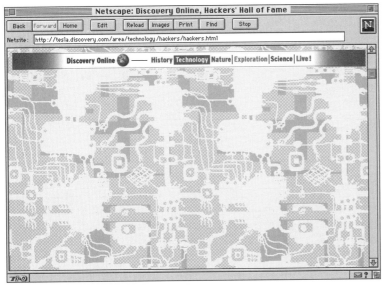

Figure 7-16. *The page for the hackers article, sans text, uses a complex image as a background*

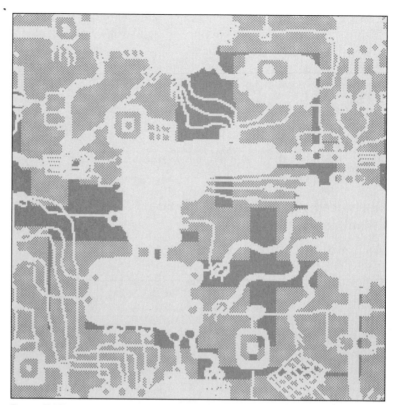

Figure 7-17. *This image creates a seamless background, thanks to the Offset filter*

Creating textured effects

You can create a texture using just about any graphic, photograph, or illustration. Figure 7-18 shows a background texture that Valerie Stambaugh created from one of my photos of sand. Starting with a crop of the photo (Figure 7-19), she lightened the image with the Brightness/Contrast controls, applied the Offset filter as described previously, and smoothed the horizontal and vertical lines that appeared in the center. The resulting background gives a nice texture to the page.

You can also create your own textures from scratch by using any number of Photoshop filters applied to a background or foreground color. Two popular filters are Photoshop's Clouds and Difference Clouds filters found under Filters: Render. If you create your texture using one of these filters and make your tile 128 × 128 or 256 × 256 pixels, it will automatically tile seamlessly. If you use these filters on images set at other dimensions, you'll need to use Photoshop's Offset filter for seamless tiles. The background in Figure 7-20 was created by applying the Clouds filter to a 128-square-pixel image.

Creating a 3D effect

You can easily create simple 3D backgrounds by using the Offset and Emboss filters. To create the background shown in Figure 7-21, Stambaugh followed these steps:

1. She created a block of 0s and 1s in Illustrator and then copied and pasted them into a 120 × 120 Photoshop file.

2. She then added a yellow background.

3. She applied the Offset filter, with values of 60, 60, Wrap Around.

4. She carefully edited the middle of the tile where the 0s and 1s didn't quite match up.

5. To create the 3D effect, she applied the Emboss filter (Filter: Stylize: Emboss).

Figure 7-19. *The original cropped image*

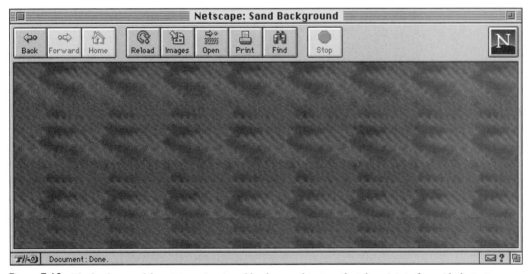

Figure 7-18. *The background for my page is a toned background texture that doesn't interfere with the text*

Another easy way to give your background a 3D look is to use the Texturizer filter found under Filters: Texture. With this filter, you have several textures to choose from, including canvas, brick, burlap, and sandstone. You can also load your own custom-made texture.

For a more complicated but very effective way to give your background a 3D effect, use the Lighting Effects filter found under Filter: Render. To create a 3D effect using this filter, you need to create a "bump" grayscale image and load it into a separate channel. This bump image can consist of a texture such as paper or sand that

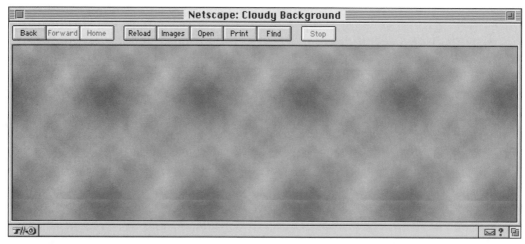

Figure 7-20. *This background tiled seamlessly without the use of the Offset filter*

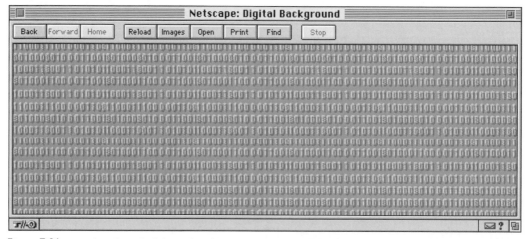

Figure 7-21. *Stambaugh applied the Emboss filter to create a 3D look for this background*

bumps light that you control with the Lighting Effects filter from its surface to produce 3D effect. Figure 7-22 shows a burlap texture created with the Texturizer. In Figure 7-23, we're using the burlap texture as a bump map with the Lighting Effects filter.

Compressing backgrounds with JPEG

Sometimes a full-size image works great as a background. The secret is to create a small file size, either through compression or careful color indexing. The next two sections present examples of backgrounds created as full-sized images.

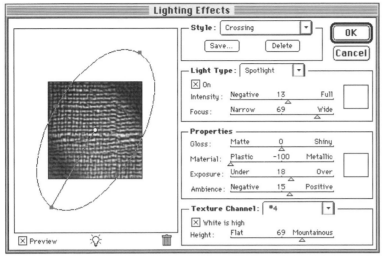

Figure 7-22. *This burlap texture was created with the Texturizer filter*

Figure 7-23. *The burlap texture is used as a bump map to create a lighting effect*

Big picture, tiny file

For my web site, Val Stambaugh turned a color photograph to grayscale as a background. Since she gave me the task of preparing the photograph, I followed these steps:

1. I converted the 580 × 580-pixel color photo to grayscale. (See Chapter 6, *JPEG: All the Color You Want*, for information about the best way to do this.)

2. Selecting the sky and clouds, I applied a Gaussian blur with a radius of 1 in order to minimize the artifacts that occur with extreme JPEG compression.

3. I lightened the entire image using the Brightness/Contrast controls so that overlaying text would be readable. The final image is shown in Figure 7-24.

4. I converted the grayscale image back to RGB so that I could use HVS JPEG, one of my favorite plug-ins.

5. Using HVS JPEG I was able to apply enough JPEG compression to reduce the file size from about 800K to about 5K! HVS JPEG allowed me to view the effects of compression in real time, and easily determine optimum file size and quality.

Although the background turns blotchy when viewed on an 8-bit monitor, I am very happy with the results. And at 5K it certainly downloads quickly enough! (Notice that I use the word "download" and not "appear." This is because the speed in which a highly compressed JPEG image decompresses varies from computer to computer, depending on the processing power of the computer.)

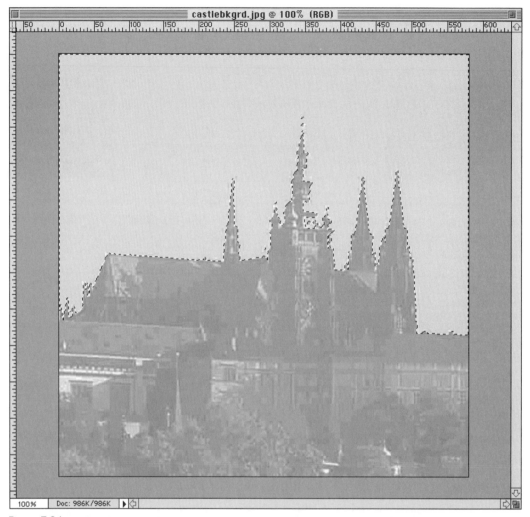

Figure 7-24. *Reduced to grayscale and heavily compressed, this 580 × 580 photograph wound up as a 5K background image*

Shakespeare as background

Steve Jablonsky of Imaginary Studios feathered the edge of the 560 × 300 Shakespeare collage shown in Figure 7-25 and saved it as a JPEG. This is the image used in the Shakespeare web site shown in Figure 7-3. Because it's a background image, the 16K image always loads in the upper left corner of the browser window, so Jablonsky can precisely position text and graphics to work with the background.

Figure 7-25. *This feathered image is used as the background for Encyclopaedia Britannica's Shakespeare site*

Grabbing backgrounds

Sometimes you might be interested in how custom backgrounds on the Web are created. If you're using Netscape for the Mac or Windows, it's easy to download the actual background tile or image itself. Once you've downloaded it, you can open it in Photoshop, examine it carefully, and through a process of trial and error, approximate the method that was used. Notice that we are not suggesting that you use the actual background itself. Using someone else's creation would be unethical (and illegal!) unless you obtain their permission.

Using Netscape on either a Mac or PC, follow these steps:

1. Once the web page containing the background has fully downloaded, choose View: Document Info. You'll see every item on the page listed. Click on Background, which should be near the top. All the statistics will show up on the bottom, including a small thumbnail version of the background itself.

2. To examine the background more closely, save the file and open it in Photoshop.

On Windows, both Netscape and Internet Explorer bring up a pop-up menu when you right-click on the background (or any other image). From here, you can view or save the image, or even set it to be your desktop wallpaper.

Another method is to go right to the source code and check the file being called from the BODY tag. Paste this location into your browser and the background file will display.

This can get a little complicated, though. For instance, if the BODY tag reads:

```
<BODY BACKGROUND="../graphics/backgd.gif">
```

and the page is located at *www.server.com/magazine/culture/music.html*, you'll need to edit the URL to read *www.server.com/magazine/graphics/backgd.gif*.

Alternatively, you can email the site you're interested in and ask them to let you know how the page was done. Many designers will be honored that you noticed their work and asked about it and will be happy to share their technique with you.

Remembering the balance

It's easy to make backgrounds with Photoshop. You can create narrow strips that tile or squares that fill the window with a pattern that you've created using any number of Photoshop filters and tools. The real challenge, however, is not technical prowess, but making an effective background that adds to your page visually without distracting from the page's content.

CHAPTER EIGHT

PHOTOSHOP WEB TYPE

There are many ways to use Photoshop to create readable, aesthetically pleasing graphic type. Although you won't have the precise control and flexibility you have with vector-oriented programs like Illustrator, Freehand, and CorelDRAW!, Photoshop's Type tool—especially with the refinements in Photoshop 4.0—gives you an effective option.

You can colorize, distort, or combine type with any number of Photoshop's filters. With the Move tool, you can precisely position type, one pixel at a time. But keep in mind that you can't edit or resize type once you place it.

With Photoshop you can easily add drop-shadow effects. And, if you're really industrious, you can even create custom bitmapped fonts.

In reality, many web designers combine a vector-based draw program and Photoshop to create type for the Web, getting the best of both worlds. In Illustrator, for example, they experiment until they find the correct size, kerning, and spacing, and then import the text into Photoshop for rasterizing, colorizing, or adding to other web graphics. Bitmapped text will look essentially the same in Photoshop as it will once it is placed on the Web.

Making readable type

When Savage Design's Bea Garcia creates graphical type for her web pages, the bottom line is readability. That means no special effects like embossing and no unnecessary colorizing that detracts from the type itself.

115

Colors and file size

Bear in mind that the need for optimal file size and browser-safe colors apply to type as well as to your other web graphics. Type is likewise ineffective if it takes a long time to download or if the colors unexpectedly shift.

Garcia consistently sets off her type from the background to ensure visibility. Typically, she uses Photoshop's Gaussian Blur filter to do this. Sometimes she applies the blur to the background behind the type, other times to a copy of the type.

She favors the Helvetica Compressed and Gill Sans fonts, especially when she needs to use smaller-sized type, because they display very well on the Web. But she uses other fonts as well. To create the type shown in Figure C-68, she chose Frutiger Bold set at 12 points. The challenge here is to make the type readable against a dark blue-green background.

Here's what she did:

1. With the Type tool selected, she clicked on the top navigational box, which was saved as a background layer. She entered her text, "Ajax Superior," selected her font and point size (12-pt. Frutiger Bold), and turned on anti-aliasing. When she clicked OK, the type was automatically placed on its own layer. (That's a new feature of Photoshop 4.0—when you place type, it automatically goes into its own separate layer, ready to be moved, colorized, scaled, rotated, or otherwise changed, but not edited or resized.)

2. She repeated this process for each navigational box, then used the Move tool to place the individual layers of text precisely.

3. With the text in place, she merged the text layers into one layer, which she named *type,* and turned off the background layer, so that only the *type* layer was visible.

4. She copied the *type* layer (choose Duplicate Layer from the Layer palette's pop-up menu), named the new layer *type shadow,* and positioned it below the *type* layer.

5. To create the drop-shadow effect, she selected the *type shadow* layer and checked the Preserve Transparency box in the Layers palette. She then filled the type with a dark gray and turned off Preserve Transparency. (Note: You can turn Preserve Transparency on and off by pressing the slash key.)

6. She applied a Gaussian blur with a radius of 1.9 pixels. (Make sure that Preserve Transparency is off before you do this or the blur won't have any effect.)

7. She merged the layers, saved it as a GIF, and placed it on the web page.

Applying a Gaussian blur to a duplicate text layer this way produces a subtle effect. But if you compare Figure C-69, which doesn't have the blur, with Figure C-70, which does, you can see that it's just enough to make the letters pop out from the green and make the reading easier for the web viewer. Such subtle differences can make all the difference on the Web.

Using layers to organize type

In Photoshop, once you place type, there is no automatic way to determine which font was used, its size, or its style. So if you want to save time when you update your web pages, it's a good idea to have a systematic plan to organize these details.

Bea Garcia has come up with a clever way to organize this information. When her page contains several typefaces, set at different sizes and styles, such as the page shown in Figure 8-1, she always creates a separate Photoshop layer where she keeps all the information regarding the type used on that particular page.

Figure 8-2 shows the layer containing this information.

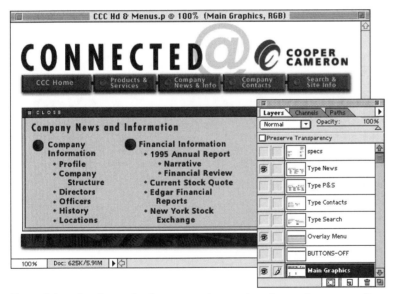

Figure 8-1. *What do you do when you can't remember what typeface you used? Save the information in a Photoshop layer.*

A simple way to make a neon effect

Corey Hitchcock at The Gate doesn't have time for fancy methods. If she uses a special effect, it has to be quick and simple. To create the neon effect shown in Figure C-71 she used Photoshop 3.0.

Incrementally moving type

In Photoshop 4.0, you can selectively move letters and words by following these steps:

1. Select the layer containing the type you wish to move, then drag with the lasso tool around the desired type or words.

2. Once you are finished selecting, activate the Move tool by pressing the keyboard letter V.

3. Position the pointer inside the selected area (or, if you are moving the contents of the entire layer without a selection, position the pointer anywhere on the screen) and drag to the desired position. To move the selection in 1 pixel increments, press Command/Control and press the arrow keys in the direction you want to go. To move the selection in 10-pixel increments, press Shift at the same time.

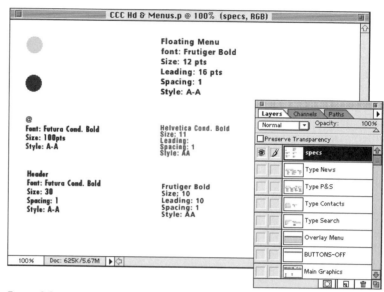

Figure 8-2. *Once you open the layer containing all the type information, it's easy to go back and make the necessary changes*

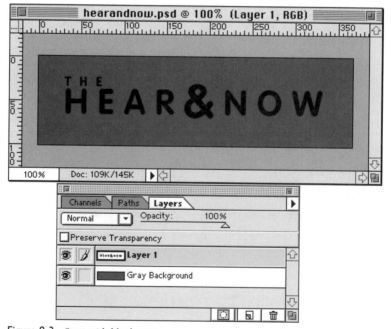

Figure 8-3. *Start with black type*

1. She created the text in Photoshop, placing it as black type, anti-
    aliased, in its own layer, against a gray background in a separate
    layer, as shown in Figure 8-3.

2. She made a copy of the layer containing the text, turned Preserve Transparency on, and filled the layer with yellow. She positioned this layer under the black text layer.

3. She turned off Preserve Transparency and applied a 4-pixel Gaussian blur to the yellow type layer, as shown in Figure C-72.

4. Then she copied the yellow layer three more times for a total of four yellow type layers. This enhanced the effects of the Gaussian blur and gave the text a neon blur, as shown in Figure C-73.

She then completed the graphic by adding a black background, a circle template she made in Illustrator, and a purple back shadow.

Pumping up your type with graphics

You can easily fill type with an illustration, texture, or even a photograph, with Photoshop 4.0's Type Mask tool. This is an easy way to embellish type and give your web page a personal look and feel. However, be sure to check your final file size. When you fill type with color-intensive photographs or illustrations, it will not only increase your file size, but also introduce colors that dither on some display systems.

Follow these steps to fill type:

1. Open the file containing the image that will fill the type. In this example, we're using a photo of a parrot, shown in Figure 8-4. Select and copy all or part of the image.

2. Create a new file for your type. Select the Type Mask tool (click and hold the Type tool to access it, as shown in Figure 8-5). Click in the window where you want to place your type. When you close the Type dialog, your type will be automatically selected and placed on its own layer, as shown in Figure 8-6. (If you try this with outlined type, only the edge of the type will be selected.) Name the layer *type*.

3. Paste the copied image into your selection (Edit: Paste Into) to create the filled type effect, shown in Figure 8-7. This places your image behind your selection; and the selection masks off the entire image except those within the type selection. When you Paste Into like this, you also create another layer, which contains both the pasted image and the image mask (shown in the Layers palette in Figure 8-7). You can move the background image by selecting the Move tool (shortcut key: V) and moving the tool within the selection area. When you have what you want, flatten the image and save it as a GIF or JPEG. The color image is shown in Figure C-74.

Adding flat colors to type

You can choose a variety of ways to apply flat color to type in Photoshop—a much easier task than creating multicolored fills. Be sure always to consider using browser colors from the Swatches palette when you colorize text. Try following these straightforward, simple steps:

- To change the color of type isolated in its own layer, select that layer, turn on Preserve Transparency, and fill the type with the foreground or background colors you want (Edit: Fill).

- To create colored type with the Type tool, select the foreground color you want before you apply the Type tool.

- You can also select type using any number of Photoshop's selection tools and fill with the Edit: Fill command.

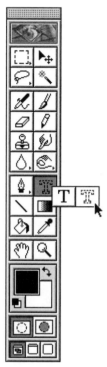

Figure 8-5. *Photoshop 4.0's Type Mask tool*

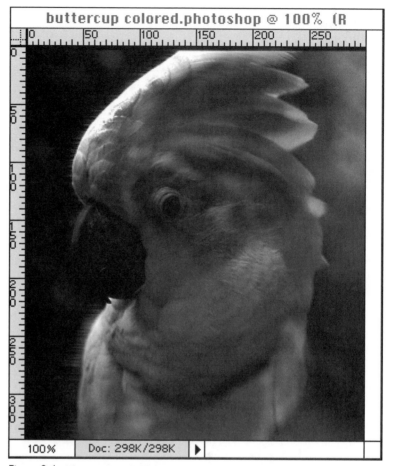

Figure 8-4. *This image will fill the type*

Graduating colors with clipped overlays

It's one thing to fill type with a single, flat color, and another to create a graduated, multicolored effect that looks good on the Web. Valerie Stambaugh put in quite a bit of effort to create the type shown in Figure C-75. Her use of clipping groups allowed her to define one layer as a mask for another layer, which gave her precise control over the way the way the type elements in the different layers interacted. It's simple to "group" layers this way (you'll see how shortly), and in the case of Valerie's work, it produced an attractive final touch without going through the effort of actually creating a mask.

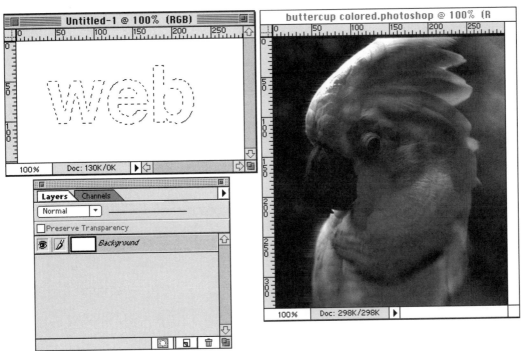

Figure 8-6. *When you use the Type Mask tool, your text appears with a selection border around it*

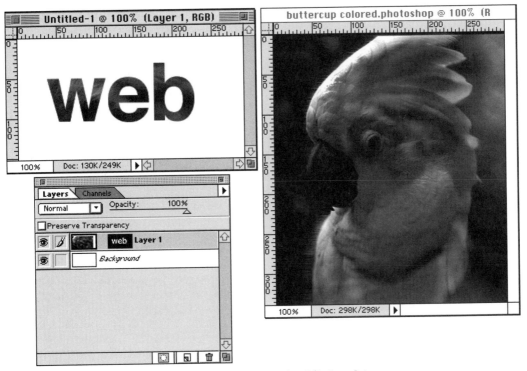

Figure 8-7. *Your image appears outlined by type when you select Edit: Paste Into*

Here's her process:

1. First she created the type in Adobe Illustrator. She used 56-point Arnold Boecklin.

2. She drag-and-dropped the Illustrator type into Photoshop 4.0, which automatically anti-aliased it and placed it on a new layer, which she named *cyber-bohemia*. (You can control whether Post-Script objects are anti-aliased or not in the File: Preferences: General dialog box. Or copy and paste, instead of drag-and-dropping, to bring up a Paste dialog box, which lets you specify whether your PostScript object will be placed as pixels or paths, and whether the pixels will be anti-aliased.)

3. Next, she created a layer for the background color. She filled this layer with the same yellow color she used for the web page background and moved it to the bottom of the stack, as shown in Figure C-76.

4. She duplicated the *cyber-bohemia* layer, named it *overlay*, and moved it to the top of the stack.

5. She selected the black type. (The easiest way to do this is to press Command/Control and click on the type layer.) Then she removed the color from the type by pressing the Delete key. The result is a transparent layer with a type selection, as shown in Figure C-77.

6. She set her foreground color to rusty red and selected the Gradient tool. Then she opened the Gradient Tool Options palette and selected the Foreground to Transparent gradient. (Since the gradient is Foreground to Transparent, it doesn't matter what your background color is at this point.) With the *overlay* layer selected she applied the gradient across the letters. (Make sure that Preserve Transparency is turned off.) The result is shown in Figure C-78.

7. To this *overlay* layer, she then applied a Gaussian blur with a radius of .5 pixels. This removed any jagged edges on the type that occurred during the blending process.

8. In the *overlay* layer, she pressed Option/Alt while clicking the cursor on the solid line separating the *overlay* and *cyber-bohemia* layers. This made a clipping group and the line became dotted. Essentially, this turned the *cyber-bohemia* layer into a mask. Now the overlay layer's texture and color appeared only in the areas defined by the letters in *cyber-bohemia*. (To unclip layers, press Option/Alt and click the line again.)

After taking care of the letterforms with clipping paths, she applied a few critical finishing touches to this graphic. With the Move tool, she added dimensionality by moving the *overlay* layer up and to the left. This simple step, combined with the effect of the clipping path, added dimensionality to the type. To see the difference, compare Figures C-79 and C-80.

She now created another duplicate of the first *cyber-bohemia* layer and named it *cyber-bohemia gaussian blur*, moving it below *cyber-bohemia*. Then she deselected the text in the *cyber-bohemia gaussian blur* layer and turned off Preserve Transparency. She applied a Gaussian blur with the radius set between 2 and 3, giving this attractive lettering a final touch.

Going that extra mile

Occasionally, you'll get that super-fastidious client who needs perfection in every detail, such as tiny, anti-aliased type. In those instances, you might need to use labor-intensive, tedious techniques, and go that extra mile.

Making tiny type

Most web designers shy away from type that is smaller than 9 points, since it's hard to read on most monitors. There are times, however, when small type is useful, as Venu's Gregg Hartling found out, so long as it is customized to be readable on the Web.

He needed something smaller than 9-point type for a web page that contained several navigational graphics all packed into a small space. Using Photoshop, he painstakingly made his own 6-point type, letter by letter. He anti-aliased the type by hand, making the tiny type very readable. These are the steps he followed:

1. With the Type tool, he created an alphabet in 9-point, upper-case, aliased Geneva to use as a model to create his tiny type.

2. Zooming in at 500%, he used the Pencil tool set at 1 pixel and carefully duplicated the model at a smaller size. Then he cut and pasted the characters to form words.

Figure 8-8 shows a sample of some of the type he created. The first and third rows are aliased 9-point Geneva; the second and fourth rows are the type he created by hand. The custom anti-aliasing effect shown here also makes the type easier to read.

Anti-aliasing by hand

When you select the Type tool's anti-alias option, Photoshop automatically adds pixels and color to simulate smooth corners instead of jaggies. But you lose control over how and which colors are used.

Choosing fonts for anti-aliasing

If you use Photoshop's anti-aliasing feature, keep in mind that some typefaces anti-alias better than others do. For example, designer Maria Yap found that the characters in a bold typeface such as Chicago get very soft and lose their integrity when anti-aliased. A more delicate font such as Geneva looks fine anti-aliased. Also, she's found that it's generally not useful to apply anti-aliasing to any type smaller than 12 points. It'll turn to mush and become difficult to read.

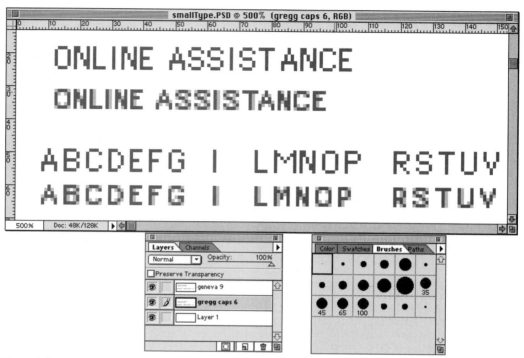

Figure 8-8. *It's quite tedious, but with Photoshop's Pencil tool you can create custom anti-aliasing of type*

With great effort, Gregg Hartling achieves an effective, anti-aliased look that gives him control. Since he uses only two browser-safe colors—one for the original type and one to create the anti-aliased look—he maintains a smaller file size and prevents unwanted dithering.

In Figure 8-8, for example, you can see where he added pixels to the letter "A" in the word *ASSISTANCE*, making it wider and more readable. Compare this with the Photoshop-generated anti-aliased type shown in Figure 8-9, and you'll understand the advantage of this method. The following steps detail his technique:

1. To have both a working and viewing window open, he opens the same file twice. This enables him to have extreme magnification in one window and see the effects of his intricate work in the other window at normal resolution.

2. Magnifying one window to at least 1200%, he picks a browser-safe color that is a darker variation of his background color. Figure 8-10 shows the window blown up to 1200%.

3. With the Pencil tool set at 1 pixel, he softens the hard edges and adds weight to an otherwise slender type.

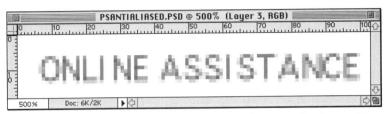

Figure 8-9. *Photoshop's anti-aliasing introduces non browser-safe colors, and in some cases makes type less readable than custom anti-aliasing*

Figure 8-10. *To improve type readability, choose a browser-safe color, then use the Pencil tool to soften hard edges and add weight to slender type*

Stroking and adding texture to type

Type on the Web that stands out can take both time and advanced Photoshop techniques, but it's worth it. To create the type shown in Figure C-81, for example, Valerie Stambaugh used a variety of techniques that gave her work a unique look. With Photoshop's Stroke command (Edit: Stroke), which uses a foreground color to paint a border around a selection, she easily created the golden outline around the words "Golden" and "The." She also used one of Photoshop 4.0's several texture tools to give the word "Alley" a nice effect.

Making the basic title elements

1. Working in Illustrator, she created the words "The Golden Alley" in the Airstream typeface, at sizes ranging from 50 to 115 points. She also created a geometrical shape to place behind the type as a unifying element. She dragged the type into Photoshop and placed it on its own layer, called *The Golden Alley*, shown in Figure 8-11.

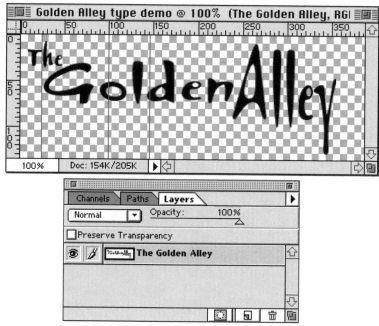

Figure 8-11. *Importing Illustrator-created type into Photoshop*

2. She brought in the geometrical shape separately, colorized it with a browser-safe gold, and named its layer *Shape*, as shown in Figure 8-12.

   She duplicated each word and placed them in separate layers so she could manipulate each word separately.

3. To create the glow around the word Golden, she switched to the appropriate layer and selected the type with the Magic Wand.

4. With a web-safe gold color selected as the foreground color, she applied a 4-pixel stroke to the selection, as shown in Figure C-82.

   To create the dropshadow, she duplicated the *Golden* layer, moved the copy beneath the original layer, and selected the new layer, called *Golden copy*.

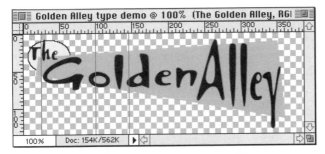

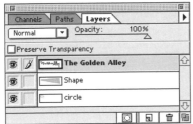

Figure 8-12. *The geometric shape is added*

5. Then she turned on Preserve Transparency, and filled the type with a web-safe rust color. With the Move tool, she offset the type down and to the right, as shown in Figure C-83.

6. In the *Alley* layer, she turned on Preserve Transparency, and filled the "Alley" type with a browser-safe pea green.

7. She then duplicated the *Alley* layer and used the Texturizer filter to apply a canvas texture. (In the Texturizer dialog, she set scaling at 120%, relief at 7 pixels, and light direction from the top.)

8. With Preserve Transparency on, she blurred the texture twice, first with a 5-pixel Gaussian blur and then with a 25-pixel motion blur. Then she applied a drop shadow, as with "Golden." Figure C-84 shows the results.

9. As with the other words, she created a drop-shadow for "The."

   On a new layer, which she placed beneath the *Shape* layer, she created an oval and filled it with an icy blue from the Web palette. Then she gave the oval a 1-pixel black stroke.

10. Using a 1-pixel-width black, she applied a stroke (Edit: Stroke), as shown in Figure C-85.

The final step is simply to turn on all the layers, index the image (using an adaptive palette to retain the texture pattern), and save it as a GIF file.

The inherent beauty of type

Virginia designer Chuck Green comes to the Web from the old school of design, where type is an artform into itself. He believes that choosing type carefully and paying attention to how individual letters interact with one another is more effective than spending hours creating some fancy effect.

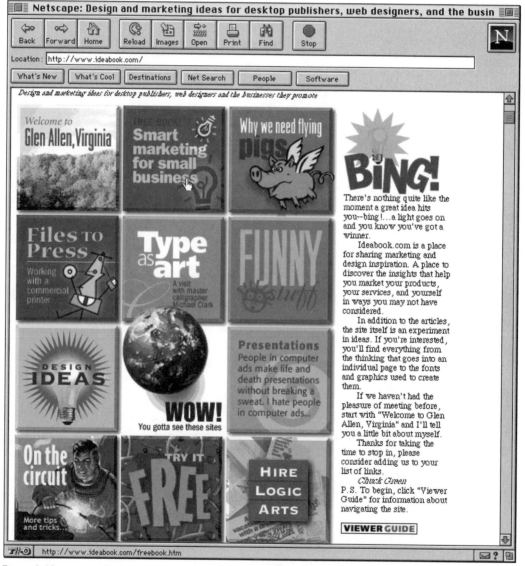

Figure 8-13. *A simple type treatment, but it shows the importance of type selection, kerning, and word spacing*

The type in Figure 8-13 was created with Photoshop 3.0 on a Windows machine. Nothing fancy was done to the type itself—no texture or distortion was applied, only an occasional flat color. Nonetheless, Chuck put a lot of thought into choosing the appropriate typefaces and positioning each letter and each word so that they related to each other in a visually appealing way.

Figure 8-14. *Green used Photoshop's Free Rotation tool to position his type*

Chuck prefers to move each type element by hand, even though Photoshop's Type tool provides a numerical way to control the amount of letter spacing and leading. Take, for example, the "Try it Free" type shown in Figure 8-14. He used Agenda Bold Ultra Condensed and Fredigor 95 Ultra Black for this graphic. He didn't do anything to the type until after he placed it with the Type tool. Then he used Photoshop 3.0's Free Rotation tool (Image: Rotate: Free) and individually moved the letters until he got them just right. He created a duplicate layer and filled the type with 50% gray, applied a slight Gaussian blur, and offset the whole layer to create a drop shadow. There's nothing fancy here, just a lot of time and patience by a very dedicated man.

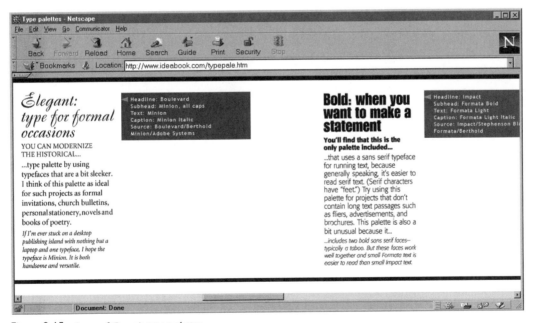

Figure 8-15. *Some of Green's type palettes*

What isn't obvious is the amount of time he spends in choosing the correct type to begin with. According to Chuck, the character of a typeface establishes a mood, much like a musical score does for a movie. It is not the primary focus, but it often plays a pivotal role in telling the story. Figure 8-15 shows two of the typeface palettes that he has put together, showing how they each elicit a particular mood or emotion. Note that each example includes a headline, a subhead, text, and a caption.

Making a difference

Even though much of the type you see on the Web is HTML-coded and never touches Photoshop, there will always be a place for graphical type. Custom-made graphical type gives your web page a unique look and feel. It also creates a visual language that helps a viewer navigate through various levels of information. If you've chosen your fonts carefully and vary the size, you can create a visual tension that holds the viewer to your page. Not only does Photoshop give you the power to create just about any special effect you want, but it also makes it easy to perform subtle tasks such as letter and word spacing that can make all the difference and show your understanding and mastery of type.

CHAPTER NINE

CREATING NAVIGATIONAL GRAPHICS

Web designers often use Photoshop to create a variety of navigational graphics, ranging from simple beveled buttons to more complex icons that contain both text and images. By taking the time to create these custom graphics, you can add a unique look and feel to your web pages that is not possible with clipart or, for that matter, simple HTML word links.

This chapter shows you quick and easy ways to spherize photographs into window-like buttons, create square buttons with beveled edges, create up and down buttons, round bullets, and forward and backward arrows, mostly through real-world examples.

Creating photo bubbles

Designer Valerie Stambaugh created the navigational device for my site, shown in Figure 9-1, by using Photoshop's Spherize filter to create bubble-shaped photographs placed in window-like buttons. Here's how she did it.

To create the Castle button on the left, she followed these steps:

1. She began by opening one of my photographs of a castle and scaling it down using Photoshop 4.0's Free Transform command (Layer: Free Transform) to the size she wanted. Holding down the Shift key to constrain the selection to a perfect circle and using the circle selection tool to select a portion of the photo, she copied and pasted the selection into a new document named *Castle Button*, pasting the image onto a white background. (see Figure 9-2). She then selected the blue background and pasted in clouds that she had copied from another photograph.

In this chapter

- Creating photo bubbles
- Creating beveled boxes with the Gradient tool
- Painting beveled buttons
- Embossing and debossing type
- Bullet balls with light effects
- Creating flashy round buttons
- Creating navigational triangles
- Using found objects
- Creating an interactive navigational bar
- Instructions in layers
- The personal touch

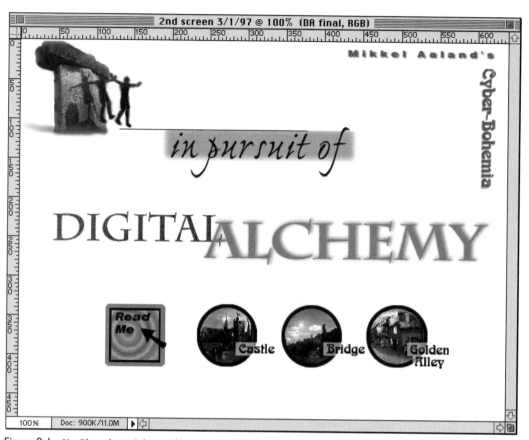

Figure 9-1. *Use Photoshop's Spherize filter on color photographs to create photo bubble navigational devices*

2. She brightened the background of the photo about 20% (Image: Adjust: Brightness: Contrast) and used the spotlight effect (Filter: Render: Lighting Effects) to bring a little more directional light into the image. To enhance the effect, she selected the lower part of the image and used Brightness/Contrast to lighten it.

3. She then selected the image area and ran the Spherize filter at 25% (normal mode).

4. After she spherized the image, she needed to tweak her lighting. She selected the image, and using the Lighting Effects filter again, she brought just a slight amount of directional light from the top right that darkened the bottom of the bubble.

5. To give the image even more of a bubble effect, she used the Burn tool to darken the bottom right corner of the circle and the Dodge tool on the top left corner of the circle. Both tools were set at 17% exposure, with Midtones selected.

6. As a final touch, she selected and stroked the bubble with a 7 pixel black border

Figure 9-2. *After selecting, copying, and pasting, the cropped photography is ready for Photoshop's Spherize filter*

She followed similar procedures to create both the Bridge and Golden Alley bubbles. Then she copied and placed all three of these images into a new file called *smaller buttons* and sized them down, as shown in Figure 9-3.

Figure 9-3. *The images after the spherizing filter and a border are applied*

To create the Read Me button, Val followed these steps:

1. She set the type in Illustrator using Berthold Akzidenz Grotesk Bold Extended, 14 point on 16 leading.

2. She then copied and pasted the type into Photoshop.

3. She drew a square with the marquee selection tool, positioned the type in the upper- left corner, then applied a black 3-pixel stroke to the square selection to make a box around the type (Edit: Stroke).

4. She created a new layer, filled it with a light blue, and used Kai's Power Tools to create the concentric circle behind the Read Me text. To mimic a computer cursor, she chose an arrow

from Zapf Dingbats and then played with this shape using Free Transform (Layer: Free Transform), sizing and rotating until she got the look of an arrow she liked.

5.   She flattened the layers, and for the final browser-safe green border, she selected the square button and stroked it 5 pixels.

When she was finished with Read Me, she aligned the four buttons on the page with the help of Photoshop 4.0's Grids feature.

To create the type for the Castle, Bridge, and Golden Alley, bubbles she did the following:

1.   Set the type (Arnold Boecklin) in Illustrator.

2.   Pasted the type over each button, using guides to position them precisely.

3.   Created a layer behind the type layer and made three identically sized rectangular selections, which she filled with 30% white so the titles would pop out but the image could still be seen behind.

Creating beveled boxes with the Gradient tool

The photo bubbles that Valerie created worked well on the opening navigational page where size wasn't critical. In order to create a smaller navigational bar for other pages, she created graphical icons and then placed them in beveled boxes that she created using the Gradient tool (see Figure 9-4).

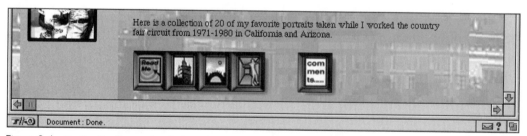

Figure 9-4. *On the Castle page, beveled graphics are compact and handy*

Here is how she made the beveled boxes:

1.   With the square marquee, she first drew a rectangular shape in Photoshop, stroking the edge 1 pixel. She then drew another rectangular shape in the center of the outer rectacle, stroked it with 1 pixel, and filled with it with 20% gray.

2. With the Line tool, she drew from the outer corner of the rectangle to each inside corresponding corner until she had a cut jewel-like shape.

3. Using the Magic Wand tool, she selected the left bevel. Using the Gradient tool she filled this selected shape with a light gray (foreground) to dark gray (background) gradient. In the Gradient Tool Options palette, she set her opacity at 100%, selected Linear, and Foreground to Background. She dragged the tool from the outer edge of her frame to the inside, holding down the Shift key to give an even fill.

4. Using the Magic Wand again, she next selected the bottom bevel and did the same as above, dragging the tool from the bottom of the bevel to the inside.

5. For the right and top bevel, she changed her blend, going from dark gray (foreground) to black (background). For the right bevel, she dragged her Gradient tool from the outer edge of her frame to the inside, and for the top bevel she dragged the tool from the top of the bevel to the inside.

She copied and pasted the button for a total of 5 buttons, as shown in Figure 9-5. Using a combination of Illustrator and Photoshop, she created the various icons that would fit inside each box. She added a 1-pixel black frame around each graphic (except for the Read Me icon), which was slightly smaller than the gray fill inside the boxes, to add a feeling of depth. (With the Golden Alley button, she pasted the figure on top of the single-pixel black frame so that it broke out over the frame, giving it more dimension.) See Figure 9-6.

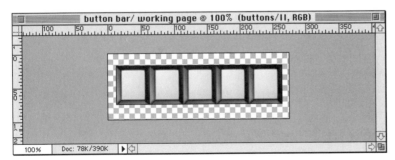

Figure 9-5. *Five beveled buttons*

To create the drop shadow, she copied the layer containing the icons, named it *blur*, and, with Preserve Transparency turned on, filled the blur copy with 50% gray. Turning off Preserve Transparency, she Gaussian-blurred it to her liking and moved the layer over and to the right, as shown in Figure 9-7. Combining these elements creates the effect seen on the web page shown in Figure 9-4.

Figure 9-6. *She added a 1-pixel frame, slightly smaller than the gray fill, to add depth to each graphic*

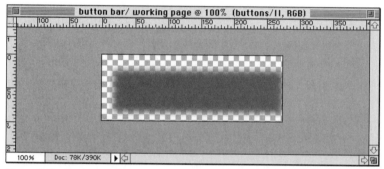

Figure 9-7. *You can make a drop shadow by applying a Gaussian blur to a duplicate layer moved slightly to the right and down*

Painting beveled buttons

Using the Gradient tool is one way to create a beveled look. Erika Sears, a full-time interactive media designer for Knowledge Adventure Software, suggests another. This method is simple, requires no filters, and relies mostly on the Paint tool.

Erika often makes her buttons "interactive," meaning that she uses Shockwave or JavaScript to make them do something when they are selected. For that reason she often creates both an "up" position and a "down" position, creating the effect of a physical button being pushed.

Here is how she creates a beveled button in the "up" position (as shown in Figure 9-8):

1. She starts with a new layer and calls it *up button.*

2. Using the Marquee selection tool, she draws a rectangle of the desired size. (Remember, you can create a square button by holding down the Shift key while you use the rectangular selection tool.)

3. She fills this selection with a color.

4. Keeping her selection active (or choosing Preserve Transparency from the Layers palette), she sets the Paintbrush to a medium-sized hard edge and "paints" the edges of the rectangle in a specific order, each with different opacities of white and black (described in the next steps).

    You can easily set your foreground to black and your back-ground to white by pressing Shift and then the letter D.

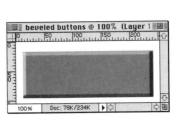

Figure 9-8. *By using the Paintbrush at different opacities, you can make an "up" button with a beveled look . . .*

5. She starts at the right side of the top edge with 50% white and her blending mode set at Normal. She holds down the Shift key and drags straight across from right to left.

6. Then for the far-left edge, she changes the opacity to 70%, holds down the Shift key and drags straight down.

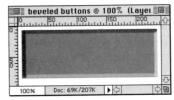

Figure 9-9. *. . . or a "down" button like this*

7. For the bottom edge, she selects black, sets her Paintbrush opacity to 50% and her blend mode to Multiply, and holding down the Shift key, she drags from left to right across the bottom edge of the rectangle.

8. For the far right edge, she also uses black, sets her opacity to 70% and her blend mode to Multiply, and holding down the Shift key, drags from top to bottom on the right edge of the rectangle.

Figure 9-10. *Create embossed type by using a white background set at 30% opacity and moved up and to the right*

To create a button in "down" position:

1. She makes a duplicate layer of the *up* button and renames it *down*.

2. She moves this duplicate rectangle to the right of the up button.

3. With the *down* layer active, she flips the button first horizontally and then vertically (Layer: Transform: Flip Horizontal/Vertical), as shown in Figure 9-9.

Embossing and debossing type

Erika also creates embossed or debossed type to represent different positions of a navigational device. To create the embossed type that you see in Figure 9-10, she did the following:

1. She created a new layer and called it *up text*.

2. She chose a black foreground and then typed in the word *button* and clicked OK to place it.

3. Using the Move tool, she positioned it over the beveled *up* button.

Figure 9-11. *Create debossed type by using a white background set at 30% opacity and moved down to the left*

4. She then selected a white foreground and typed in the word *button* and clicked OK to place it.

5. She changed the opacity of the layer containing the white text to 30%.

6. She used the arrow keys to position the white text slightly up and to the right of the black button type. This gives it an embossed look.

To give the same type a debossed look, she repeated the same process, but in step 6 she positioned the white text over the black text slightly down and to the left, as shown in Figure 9-11.

Bullet balls with light effects

Bullet balls come in handy as a way to separate large blocks of text and provide an intuitively recognized navigational button. Here are a couple of ways that Erika creates them.

To create the ball of the type shown in Figure 9-12:

1. She draws a circle on a new layer with the circular Marquee, holding down the Shift key to make a perfect circle.

2. She fills this selection with color.

3. She uses the Lens Flare filter (Filter: Render: Lens Flare). Options set: Brightness 85%, Lens Type 105mm Prime.

4. To keep the gradation intact, she converts to Indexed Color mode and selects 8-bit adaptive diffusion.

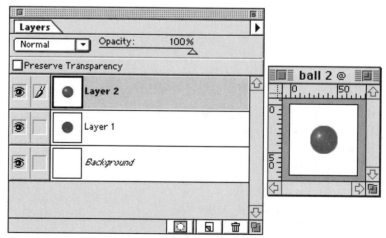

Figure 9-12. *Sears created this bullet ball with Photoshop's Lens Flare filter*

To create a ball like the one shown in Figure 9-13:

1. She uses the circular Marquee on a new layer to create a circle.

2. She sets the Gradient tool options to Radial, 100% Foreground to Background (with her foreground set to white and her background set to a desired color), dragging a short line from left to right at a 45-degree angle, creating a highlight.

3. To keep the gradation intact, she converts to the Index mode and selects 8-bit adaptive diffusion.

Creating flashy round buttons

Here is another method Erika uses to create round buttons that are a bit flashier and can be made in an "up" or "down" position.

To create "up" position buttons as the one shown in Figure 9-14, Erika does the following:

1. Makes a new layer called *base up*.

2. Uses the circle Marquee tool to draw a circle the size of her desired button.

3. Selects two colors, a light foreground (preferably white) and a dark background.

4. Uses the Gradient tool set at Linear and Foreground to Background with 100% gradation and drags it straight across the middle of the circle from the left edge to the right edge.

5. Makes a new layer and calls it *top up*.

6. Draws a smaller circle to fit within the larger one. (The edges of the big one should be wide and visible.)

7. Changes the Gradient tool setting to Radial, and keeps 100% opacity.

8. Drags the Gradient tool across the middle of the circle from the left to right starting in about one-quarter of the total diameter.

9. Positions this circle on top of the larger one on the layer below.

10. Fills the center ball with a color, setting her opacity to 100% and her Mode to Soft Light.

To create "down" position buttons such as the one shown in Figure 9-15:

1. Erika duplicates the layers she called *base up* and *top up* and calls them *base down* and *top down*.

2. She then merges *top up* and *base up*.

Figure 9-13. *Sears created this bullet ball with Photoshop's Gradient tool*

Figure 9-14. *A button in the up position*

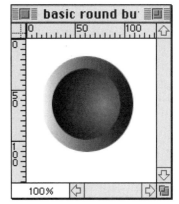

Figure 9-15. *A button in the down position*

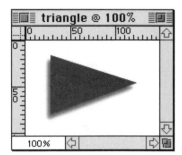

Figure 9-16. *A triangle created using Photoshop's Pen tool*

3. She moves this newly merged button to the right to see the objects below.

4. Then she rotates the smaller circle in the *top down* layer 180 degrees (Layer: Transform: Rotate 180 degrees).

5. Then she merges the *top down* and *base down* layers.

6. As a final step, she fills the center ball called *top down* with a color ink, setting the opacity to 100% and mode to Multiply.

Creating navigational triangles

Triangles always make good navigation devices, and they are very easy to create using Photoshop. Here is one way that Erika creates triangles such as the one shown in Figure 9-16:

1. First, she creates a new layer.

2. Then she selects the Pen tool from the Toolbox and uses it to draw a triangle. (To use this tool, position the pointer where you want the first point of the triangle to begin. Click to define an anchor point. Then reposition your pointer to the second point of the triangle, click, and a straight line between the first and second points will appear. Do this again for the third point of the triangle.

   Create the final line of the triangle by clicking back on the first point that you created.)

3. She saves this as a path by selecting Save Path from the Paths palette menu.

4. She makes a selection from her path by choosing Make Selection from the Paths palette menu, leaving her Feather Radius set to 0, and chooses Anti-aliased. Once she makes her selection, she deletes the path in the Paths palette.

5. She then fills the remaining selection with a color. If you haven't deleted the original path an outline of the path will be visible on the parameter of the filled triangle. (Note: you can also fill your initial path by choosing Fill: Path from the Paths palette menu, but you won't get a smooth edge.)

6. To make a drop shadow, she duplicates the layer containing the triangle and places this layer underneath the layer containing the original triangle.

7. Then she feathers the selected duplicate triangle 2 pixels and fills the selection with 100% black. She sets her layer opacity to 50% from the Layers palette options pull-down menu. When she is finished, she merges the layers.

Using found objects

With a little help from Photoshop just about anything can be digitized and turned into a web navigational device.

Mobile buttons

"Turbo" Ted's work, as you can see in Figure 9-17, is a visual cacophony. He shies away from using text, using instead pictures and graphics readable in Japan as well as in Russia. His ultimate test is his newborn baby. If the baby responds to the material he puts on his web page, well, it works.

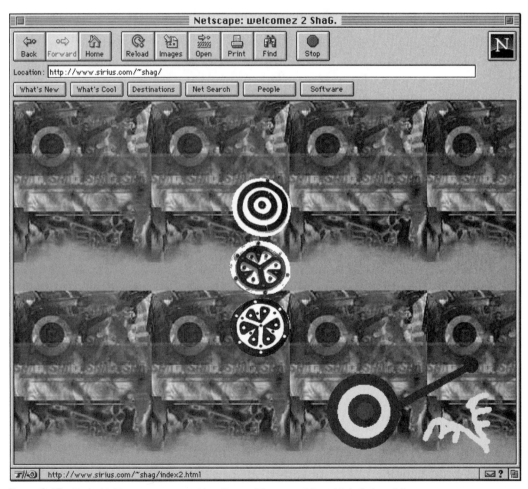

Figure 9-17. *Turbo Ted's opening page with a "button" he created from his baby's mobile*

To this end, Turbo photographed his newborn's black and white mobile with a digital camera, and using Photoshop transformed the photos into a series of images that animate and link to other pages.

To create web navigational devices from real-life objects, he followed these steps:

1. He used a digital camera to shoot his child's black-and-white mobile. Figure 9-18 shows one of the original camera shots.

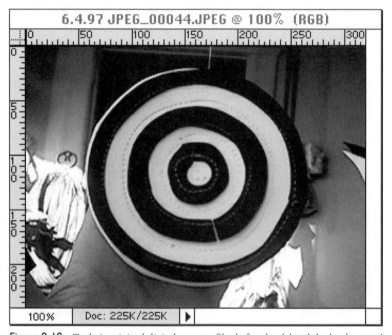

Figure 9-18. *Turbo's original digital camera files before he deleted the background*

2. He removed the background using the Pen tool. He did this by carefully outlining the pertinent parts of the image, making a path from the Paths palette, and then turning the path into a selection and deleting it.

3. He filled the background selections with green, a color he chose to be transparent when he indexed (Image: Mode: Indexed Color) and converted his images to GIFs (see Figure 9-19).

4. Then he scaled the photos down (Image: Image Size).

5. He indexed his images using the Adaptive palette with no dither. Finally, he created a GIF, designating the background as transparent.

Figure 9-19. *After the background was deleted, Turbo filled the background with green, which he would later designate as transparent*

Figure 9-20. *Sears created the paper buttons from scratch*

Scrap buttons

To create the scrap paper button icons shown in Figure 9-20, Erika Sears:

1. Scanned a scrap piece of paper at 72-ppi grayscale.

2. She adjusted the brightness and contrast (Image: Brightness/ Contrast) to achieve the right highlights.

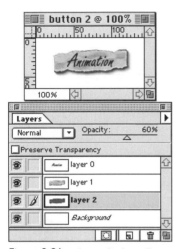

Figure 9-21. *She applied a yellow tint, drop shadow, and text to the scanned paper*

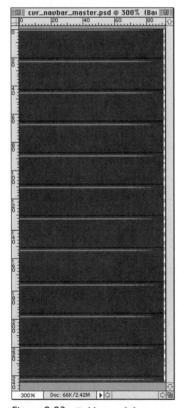

Figure 9-23. *Bobby used the Gradient tool and the Line tool to create these lines*

3. She placed this scrap on *layer 1* and then created a duplicate image below on *layer 2*.

4. To make a drop shadow she selected and feathered (Select: Feather) this duplicate image 2 pixels, filled with black, and set the blending opacity at 60%.

5. She gave the scrap paper on *layer 1* a tint by selecting and filling it with yellow, using the Multiply mode at 100%.

6. She then created the type using Photoshop's Type tool, and placed it on *layer 0* positioned over the scrap paper layers. See Figure 9-21.

Creating an interactive navigational bar

MSNBC's Bobby Stevens created the complex navigational bar shown in Figure 9-22 using 29 layers filled with 11 buttons, drop-shadowed text, and a simulated dithered edge. Because the design called for the navigational bar to change colors when buttons were selected or "rolled over," Bobby had to build in extra layers for different colors as well.

Figure 9-22. *The navigational bar to the left, created entirely in Photoshop, changes colors when the cursor rolls over a button, or when that button is active*

He created this high-tech navigational bar by following these steps:

1. He created a new file measuring 92 × 244 pixels, a dimension given to him by the programmers at MSNBC.

2. He filled the background layer with a browser-safe gray.

3. Measuring the rectangle into 11 equal parts, he used the Gradient and Line tools to draw two horizontal lines. He created the light line shown in Figure 9-23 (blue in the color version) with the Gradient tool (with two different shades of blue selected as the foreground and background colors and the gradient set to a linear, foreground-to-background blend). Above that line he created a 1-pixel aliased black line using the Line tool.

4. He then selected the area above and including the lines, and copied and pasted the button so that he had eleven identical buttons, which he included as part of his background.

5. On one layer, he set all the type in Photoshop using Meta Bold type, anti-aliased. He selected and positioned all the type by hand, using guides to set the type 3 pixels in from the left and 2 pixels down from the blue line.

6. He then duplicated the type layer and made a drop shadow. Then he merged the two layers into one layer, as shown in Figure 9-24.

7. He then created a 92 × 19-pixel selection (the size of each button) on a new layer, and filled that selection with a browser-safe blue. He duplicated that layer eleven times and then dragged each color bar into a position over each button. (The blue shows a web user that the selection is active.)

8. To create the teal color that appears when the user passes the cursor over the button, Bobby simply duplicated his blue button, and with Preserve Transparency on in his Layers palette, he filled the blue area with teal. (The rollover effect was programmed by MSNBC programmers using ActiveX technology. Bobby was able to approximate the final programming effect by turning his Photoshop layers off and on.)

9. Bobby's last step was to create the dither on the right side of the bar. With the Pencil tool, he drew a 2-pixel wide vertical line. Then he went in by hand and used the Pencil tool to add the pixels you see in Figure 9-25, extending them no more than 9 pixels in. It took a lot of experimentation to get an effect that looked right on a variety of platforms and monitors.

Figure 9-24. *Text with a shadow all on one layer*

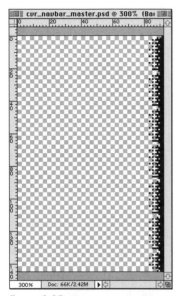

Figure 9-25. *Bobby created this simulated dither look with the Pencil tool and a lot of hard work*

Instructions in layers

Figure 9-26 shows yet another example of how a Photoshop layer can be used to provide a very specific set of instructions that always remains with the Photoshop file. In this particular example, MSNBC designer Bobby Stevens included instructions to fellow designers on how to create section banners. Other repeating elements were specified this way as well. This made it simple for Bobby to hand off work and not have to answer endless questions about how repeating elements were created. Notice the click points for aligning type precisely and the color swatch for easy sampling.

The personal touch

In this chapter, we've outlined very specific ways to create navigational graphics. When you follow our step-by-step examples, keep in mind that you can easily add your own personal touch in many ways. For example, when color is called for, most of the time you can add any color. Size too can be altered to fit both the content of the navigational graphic and the needs of your web page.

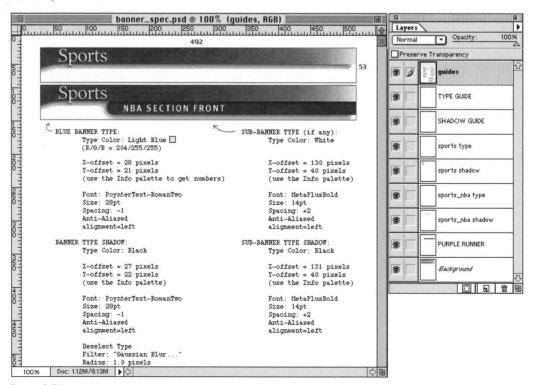

Figure 9-26. *You can readily find all the information about a particular graphic when it is contained in one Photoshop layer*

CHAPTER TEN

IMPORTING VECTORS INTO PHOTOSHOP

At some point in the web design process, there is a good chance that you'll use a drawing program such as Illustrator, FreeHand, or CorelDRAW! These vector-based programs are quite good for creating text and complex illustrations, because they use mathematical equations to define resolution-independent shapes and lines. Photoshop and other bitmap programs, on the other hand, use a limited number of discrete pixels to make up an image.

Since the Web is a bitmap environment, all vector-based graphics must ultimately be "rasterized" or converted to bitmaps. Typically, newer draw programs provide ways of rasterizing vector graphics into bitmaps. Still, you'll likely find it convenient to import vector images into Photoshop and let Photoshop convert from vectors to bitmaps, as shown in Figure 10-1. Photoshop does an excellent job of converting vector-based graphics into bitmaps, and you can also combine your converted vector graphic with other Photoshop-created elements. By using Photoshop as a web layout tool, you can get an idea of how all pieces interact with each other on the page.

This chapter shows you how web designers bring vector-based drawings into Photoshop, as well as how they work around some of the problems such as color shifts that occur when transferring files between vector-based programs and Photoshop.

In this chapter

- Importing vector files
- Avoiding color shifts
- Two are better than one

Importing vector files

Regardless of which drawing program you use, the process of bringing vector-based graphics into Photoshop is pretty straight forward. The method you use depends on which drawing program you use and the degree of control you seek over how a graphic is placed. For example, if you use File: Place, you can precisely resize any EPS graphic saved in the Illustrator format before it is converted

Save in EPS

If you plan to open a graphic that you have created in Illustrator, Free-Hand, or CorelDRAW! in Photoshop, it's best to save your graphic in the Illustrator EPS file format and let Photoshop do the actual rasterizing. You can also save your file as a TIFF and open it in Photoshop, but the results won't be as good as if you use the Illustrator format, which is supported by most drawing programs.

Regardless of which program you use, keep in mind that if the file contains layers, they'll be flattened into one layer when the file is opened in Photoshop. This is downright inconvenient, because without layers containing the individual shapes, objects, and lines of your graphic, it is more difficult to colorize and otherwise handle the image. (For a workaround to this problem, see the section "Working with Painter.")

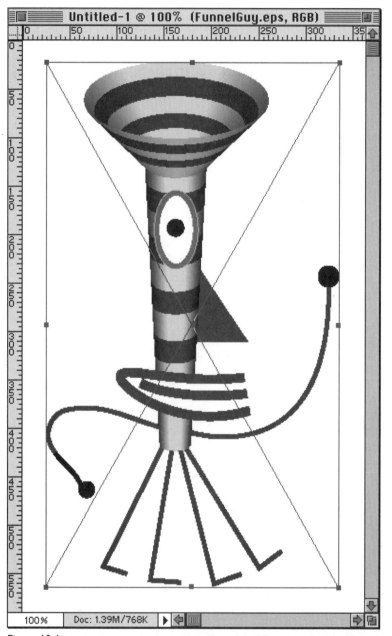

Figure 10-1. *Importing a vector image into Photoshop (illustration by John Hersey)*

to bitmap. If you copy and paste, you'll get to choose whether to paste vectors as pixels or paths. If you drag and drop from a program that supports this method, you won't be presented with any options at all. Photoshop will automatically rasterize and size the copied item for you.

Working with Illustrator

Customarily, Brian Frick of Discovery creates his web pages using a combination of Illustrator and Photoshop. Producing the basic shapes in Illustrator, he brings his work into Photoshop, where he combines it with bitmap figures and adds the final colors.

Why does he add the colors in Photoshop? Brian has learned that when colors are brought from Illustrator to Photoshop they aren't accurately reproduced. A green in Illustrator might look blue and washed out in Photoshop because of the different ways the two programs handle color. (Although Illustrator 7.0 works in the same RGB color mode as Photoshop, it also has a color-shifting problem, albeit not as extreme as earlier versions.) So there is little reason for him to spend time on color in Illustrator—rather, he concentrates on ways to bring his Illustrator files into Photoshop so that it is easy to colorize the separate parts.

The secret to this is placing each component of his illustration in a separate Photoshop layer. Figure 10-2 shows how he can then easily use each layer to fill or paint colors precisely where he wants them.

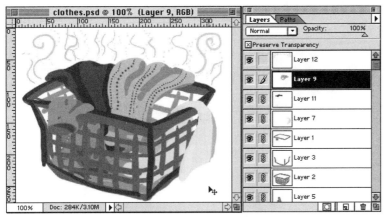

Figure 10-2. *You can easily colorize each object of an illustration when each object is placed in its own Photoshop layer*

When he is working with an illustration containing only a few objects to colorize, Brian either drags and drops or copies and pastes each object into a Photoshop layer. (Either of these two methods can apply to a FreeHand or CorelDRAW! graphic as well, depending on the particular version of the program.) He generally sets his preferences so the objects come in anti-aliased. (If you want to ensure that no new colors are introduced, bring your graphic in aliased.)

These methods are fine so long as there are only a few objects to copy and paste or drag and drop. For complex illustrations, Brian resorts to his own workaround with Fractal Design Painter, a best-selling paint program that works with both vector and bitmapped graphics. Using this workaround (described in the next section), he can bring an Illustrator file into Photoshop with all its layers intact.

Occasionally, Brian opens his Illustrator EPS file directly into Photoshop. Because this process flattens all the Illustrator layers and makes it harder to colorize the individual objects, he does this only with very simple illustrations where fine-tuning the colors is not necessary.

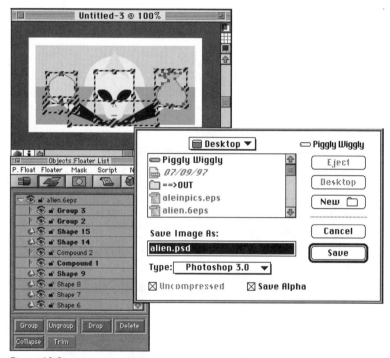

Figure 10-3. *In Painter, Brian saves his Illustrator file with its layers intact as a Photoshop 3.0 document*

Working with Painter

It's a tedious process to copy and paste or drag and drop objects from an Illustrator file into individual, separate Photoshop layers. In an ideal world you would be able to simply open the Illustrator file in Photoshop with all the layers intact. Since that isn't the case, you might follow this clever workaround discovered by Brian Frick. If you already have Painter, it won't cost you a thing. If not, the program goes for a street price of around $300. It's definitely worth the price if you have a lot of Illustrator files needing bitmap conversion. It's also a very good paint program.

To convert bitmaps with Painter, Brian follows these steps:

1. He saves his work as an Illustrator file.

2. Importing the file into Painter, he does nothing to it except choose Save As. Painter gives him the option of saving in Photoshop 3.0 format, which he does, as shown Figure 10-3.

3. Now when he opens the file in Photoshop, it opens with all the original Illustrator layers intact and in order, so he can proceed to colorize each object. See Figure 10-4.

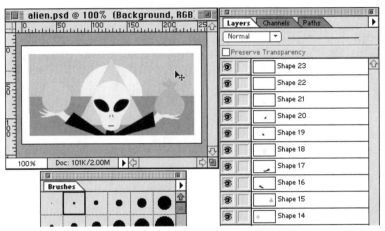

Figure 10-4. *Once Brian opens the file in Photoshop, all the layers are intact and in order, and he proceeds to colorize each of the individual objects*

The final result of Brian's effort as it appeared on a Discovery site is shown in Figure 10-5.

Brian used this technique with both Painter 4.0 and Painter 5.0 with good results.

Working with FreeHand

At Icon Medialab in Madrid, Johan Thorngren is a web designer who often creates and converts existing corporate logos for the Web. Starting in FreeHand, he copies and pastes aliased objects into Photoshop for the final rasterizing and colorizing.

His best results occur when he imports the aliased logo at its maximum size and then incrementally resizes it (50%) to the appropriate size.

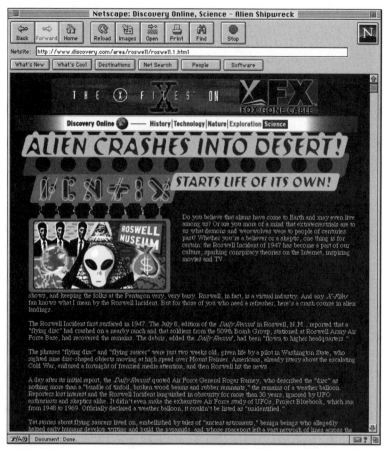

Figure 10-5. *Brian's final illustration as part of a Discovery web page*

Here is how he created the logo shown in Figure 10-6:

1. In FreeHand, he created the black logo on a white background.

2. He copied and pasted the entire aliased FreeHand drawing into Photoshop and placed it into its own layer.

3. He resized the graphic in Photoshop (Image: Image Size) to reduce the size of the graphic and to simulate an anti-aliased look. By keeping his interpolation setting at Bicubic and incrementally scaling down the logo 50% at a time, he achieved a controlled anti-aliased effect. You can set the interpolation setting in the Image Size dialog box, or in Preferences.

    (As covered in Chapter 1, *Making Photoshop Web-Friendly*, the Bicubic setting adds data and color when needed; hence the smooth edges in Thorngren's graphic. If you want to keep the jagged aliased look, you should set your interpolation setting to Nearest Neighbor; you'll need to reset this each resizing.)

Figure 10-6. *By bringing in a vector graphic as big as you can and resizing it in Photoshop in increments of 50%, you'll get excellent results, as Johan Thorngren did with the logo shown here*

4. He colored the logo in Photoshop by using the Magic Wand with settings at 0 tolerance and "aliased" to select the white background. He deleted the white to transparent, leaving only the black logo on its own layer. Selecting that layer he chose Preserve Transparency, then selected a browser-safe color, which he applied to the logo by holding down Option/Alt and the Delete key. (This fills the pixels in the layer with the foreground color.)

5. He saved the graphic as a GIF and combined it on a page with the other graphic elements. (The outline and texture for the bubbles were created in a 3D program while the "lens" effect was hand-painted in Photoshop.)

Avoiding color shifts

Whatever method you use to bring a vector graphic into Photoshop, you need to be aware of the inevitable, and for the most part, unpredictable color shifts that occur when moving graphics between these different programs. You have several choices of what to do about this problem, including the following:

- Ignore the color shifts, figuring most people use lousy monitors and won't appreciate your attention to detail anyway.

- Use the Paint Bucket, Fill, or another Photoshop technique to colorize all or part of your illustration and increase contrast or boost color saturation.

- Use the workaround suggested by Adobe (described in detail in the section "Adobe's solution to color shifting" later in this chapter) to calibrate the way Illustrator and Photoshop apply colors.

- Work in your drawing program with the limited browser-safe color palette. This may give you better results than if you added color willy-nilly, but even browser-safe colors shift when brought into Photoshop. You'll still need to apply Photoshop color carefully to your work.

Bumping up contrast and color saturation

Illustrator John Hersey has an immensely sensible attitude toward color on the Web. Basically, he doesn't worry too much about it. That's fine for him because most of his work is personal and stylized. He starts out in either Illustrator or FreeHand and uses any color he wants. Much of his work is destined for print, so he's often working in the CMYK color mode. When he brings his illustrations over to Photoshop using the copy and paste technique, he looks to see if there were any radical changes in the color. If not, he leaves it alone.

Often his Illustrator or FreeHand colors seem washed out and dull. He uses Photoshop's contrast and saturation controls to enhance the color. It doesn't matter whether it matches the original colors as long as it looks good to him. Sometimes, he replaces an entire background color with a browser-safe color from his color swatch palette.

Filling shapes with color

In Photoshop, Brian Frick uses two techniques to colorize his Illustrator work. The first technique fills the shape to the parameter, leaving a black line, and creating what he calls a grunge look. The second technique results in a colored shape with no discernible border.

Creating a grunge look

To create the grunge look, as shown in Figure 10-7, he followed these steps:

1. In Illustrator, Brian created a graphic with black lines and imported it to Photoshop. (He could have just as easily created the simple graphic in Photoshop, but he wouldn't have been able to go back later and adjust or change the lines like he can in Illustrator.)

2. He filled the graphic with the Paint Bucket. As shown in the magnified view in Figure 10-8, the color goes only to the edge of the black line, and because it is anti-aliased, it leaves a slight halo, providing the visual effect he wanted.

Figure 10-7. *Use the Paint Bucket to fill an outline with color*

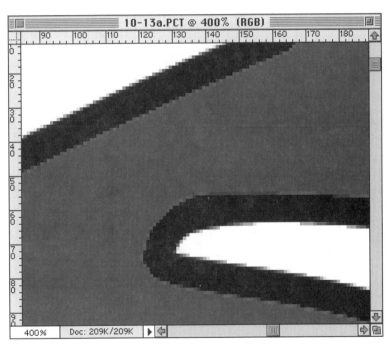

Figure 10-8. *When you fill an anti-aliased shape with the Paint Bucket, a halo effect results*

Creating a colored shape

Figure 10-9 shows the effect of colorizing individual objects placed in their own layers with Preserve Transparency turned on. When Brian uses this method, Photoshop's Fill command and other paint methods colorize the Illustrator-created lines as well, resulting in a shape of color rather than an outline filled with color.

To create a "borderless" colored shape, he followed these steps:

1. In Illustrator, Brian created the basket and its contents and imported it to Photoshop, placing each element in its own layer.

2. Selecting one layer at a time he chose browser-safe colors and with Preserve Transparency selected he filled each layer with color. He then went back and added more colors for texture and odor "fumes" with the paintbrush.

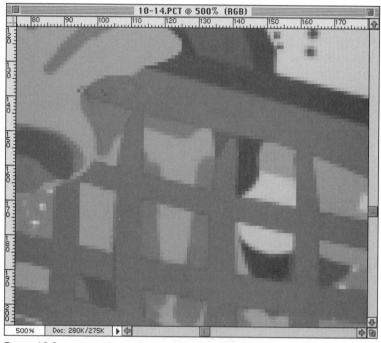

Figure 10-9. *When a shape is in its own layer, with Preserve Transparency turned on, the Fill command completely fills the shape, including the black outline*

Adobe's solution to color shifting

Adobe suggests a way to minimize the color shift that occurs when you transfer files between Illustrator and Photoshop. Their method actually attempts to calibrate the two programs to a common color specification. It certainly improves the way Photoshop handles Illustrator files, but it is by no means a perfect solution. Colors still shift unexpectedly. However, if you want to avoid the time-consuming hassle of colorizing an Illustrator file in Photoshop, you can at least minimize shifts by creating and loading a color table. To create the table, follow these steps:

1. Create an Illustrator file with seven boxes. Fill the boxes with the color mixes shown in Table 10-1.

Table 10-1. *Values for Color Table*

Box	Cyan	Magenta	Yellow
1	100%		
2		100%	
3			100%
4		100%	100%
5	100%		100%
6	100%	100%	
7	100%	100%	100%

2. Leave this window open. Open Photoshop, but don't open any files.

3. Choose File: Color Settings: Printing Inks Setup in Photoshop.

4. Choose Custom from the Ink Colors pop-up menu.

5. To compare colors, align this dialog box as close as possible to the Illustrator window. Then follow these steps:

   — In the Printing Inks Setup dialog, click the Cyan box. The Color Picker opens.

   — Adjust the color until it matches the Illustrator window that contains Box 1.

   — Click OK.

6. Repeat step 5 for each of the seven color boxes. All of them should match the colors you see in the Illustrator window. Click OK to adopt these colors and to return to the Printing Inks Setup dialog.

7. Click Save at the Printing Inks Setup dialog and name your custom ink setup file *Illustrator Colors*. Click OK.

Once you've created this color profile, you can load it in Photoshop by following these steps:

1. Open Photoshop. (Don't open the Illustrator file yet!)

2. Choose File: Color Settings: Printing Inks Setup in Photoshop.

3. Click Load to load the file named *Illustrator Colors*. Click OK.

4. Choose File: Open to select an Illustrator file. Change the mode to RGB. Click OK.

5. The file should now look the same as it did in Illustrator.

Two are better than one

This chapter has shown you some techniques web designers have used to expand the capabilities of Photoshop. When you combine the features of drawing programs with Photoshop, you need a strategy to deal with the likely color shifts. But keep in mind that the resulting dynamic web pages will be well worth the effort.

CHAPTER ELEVEN

LAYING OUT PAGES IN PHOTOSHOP

More and more web designers are using Photoshop as a web design tool—with good reason. With Photoshop, you can comp pages, place text and images, and finesse your design before going to the trouble of saving numerous files and creating the page in HTML.

Unlike most layout applications, Photoshop is a bitmap program, meaning that what you see on your monitor is usually a good approximation of what others will see on theirs. With Photoshop's layers feature, you can quickly turn individual graphical elements on and off to see how they relate to each other. With Photoshop's guides, grids, and snap-to features, you can precisely align type and graphics just as you would in a traditional layout program. If you use animations in your work, you can even create a Photoshop 4.0 Action that simulates the animated sequence.

Of course, you still need to convert your graphics to an appropriate file format and use HTML code to place them on the Web. Photoshop is good, but not that good! Think of the Photoshop display the same way you think of an Iris print—it's a visual record of what you want your page to look like when all is said and done.

This chapter includes profiles of several web designers who use Photoshop as a layout tool. You'll see how they use guides, grids, and layers to break up complex graphics for optimal downloading and quality.

You'll also learn the basics of creating and using Photoshop 4.0's guides and grids, and how to set up a web page template. Since earlier versions of Photoshop don't offer guides and grids, we'll go through how to create them using layers and drawing tools.

In this chapter

- Painting design on a web page
- Redesigning with layers and grids
- Animating your graphics with Actions
- Using guides to design and crop
- Keeping boundaries with templates
- Working within the "live" area
- Coding layout information in a layer
- Unintended uses

Layers 101

Photoshop's layer capabilities—available in Version 3.0 and higher—are what makes Photoshop such an effective web layout tool, and a great web production program in general.

Layers allow you to place individual objects on individual transparent layers, and through different opacity and blending modes, control the way they interact. You can work with as many as 100 layers, limited mostly by the memory capabilities of your machine.

Here are some of the more important things you should know about layers that will help you use Photoshop as a web layout tool and as a web production program in general.

Creating and deleting layers

As you build your web page, you'll constantly be adding and deleting layers—whether you mean to or not.

If you want to create a new layer—for example, to store vital production information about your page—you can simply click on the New Layer icon at the bottom of the palette, or choose New Layer from the Layers palette pop-up menu. In Photoshop 4.0, you can also choose Layer: New from the menu bar.

Selected layers can be deleted by dragging a layer to the trashcan icon on the Layers palette, selecting a layer and clicking on the trashcan, or selecting Layer: Delete Layer from the menubar (Photoshop 4.0 only).

In Photoshop 4.0, every time you paste an object from another file into your active file, or use the Type tool, Photoshop automatically creates a new layer. (In Photoshop 3.0, the pasted selection or placed type comes in as an active floating selection; to place it on its own layer, you have to choose Make Layer from the Layers palette drop-down menu. Make Layer is an option only when you paste.)

In 4.0, it's easier than ever to create a new layer by converting a selection: simply make your selection, then under the Layers menu choose New: Layer Via Copy.

Making layers visible and invisible

One of the great advantages of layers is that you can hide parts of the image, so you can work on other parts. To hide layers, just click the eye icon in front of the layer you want to make invisible. To show them, click again. This process can quickly turn tedious if you have 50 layers and you want to show only one. To turn off all layers except the selected layer, hold down Option/Alt and click the eye icon. When you want to turn the other layers back on, simply repeat this process.

Making layers active

In order to work on an object, its layer must be active. Only one layer can be active at a time. You can make it active by simply clicking on the desired layer in the Layers palette or, if you are using the Move tool, you can actually select a layer from within the image window itself. To do this,

→

place the Move tool over the object you wish to make active, then hold the Command/Control key while you click. A drop-down menu will appear, giving you the choice of making this the active layer. You can tell that a layer is active when it is highlighted in the Layers palette. This method is particularly useful when you are trying to position lots of type on different layers since it saves you the effort of going back and forth between the Layers palette and the image window.

Preserve Transparency

When you select Preserve Transparency from the Layers palette, you will be able to edit only the areas of the layer that contain pixels. This can be very useful or very annoying, depending on what you are trying to do. For example, if you use the Type tool, select Preserve Transparency, and then choose Edit: Fill, only the type itself will change to your selected color. However, let's say you want to apply a Gaussian blur to that same type. You'll quickly see that the filter doesn't have the effect that you wanted. With Preserve Transparency selected, pixels are "contained," and the Gaussian blur won't apply to anything outside the initial boundaries.

Creating special effects using layers

Layers aren't only great for organizing graphics; they can help facilitate special effects as well. Many of the effects mentioned throughout this book rely on the use of the Blending and the Opacity options in the Layers palette—options that determine the way that pixels in adjacent layers interact.

Flattening layers

When you are ready to convert your work to a file format supported by the Web, you will have to flatten the layers, since only the Photoshop format understands layers. From the Layers palette drop-down menu, choose Flatten Image. When you save the file, choose Save As to keep your original Photoshop file with the layers intact for future changes.

Painting design on a web page

Washington D.C.-based graphic designer Valerie Stambaugh used Photoshop 4.0 to create the pages for my personal web site, *cyberbohemia.com.*

Stambaugh applies her background as a painter/printmaker to page layout. She often builds her pages in much the same way that she paints on canvas when she is employing the "Old Master" technique. This technique involves sketching out the composition in black and white or a dark color first. Then composition and balance are resolved. Layout in color comes last. Figure 11-1 is a page she designed utilizing this method.

Valerie normally works with Quark for her print projects, but she finds working with Photoshop refreshing. "It's much more like painting," she says, pointing to the ability of Photoshop to turn

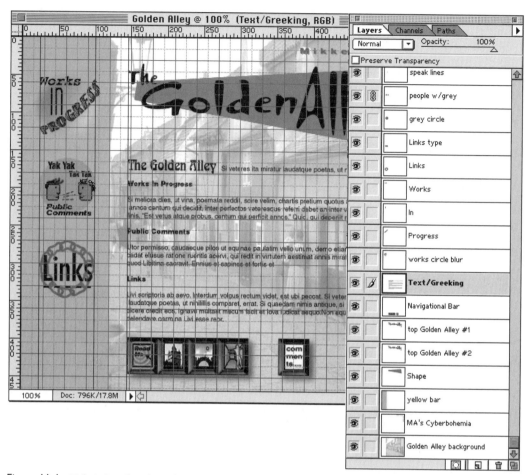

Figure 11-1. *Valerie Stambaugh works mostly in black in white, adding color later, and aligns graphical elements with Photoshop's guides*

layers off and on and view the results immediately. She uses grids occasionally—mostly to kern or to align type—but she finds grids a bit distracting. Instead, she usually creates guides as she needs them to align objects.

When Valerie is finished with a page (such as the one in Figure 11-1), she often passes the actual HTML work on to a colleague. She always sends the complete Photoshop file, with layers intact, as a page proof so there is never any doubt about the way she wants things to look.

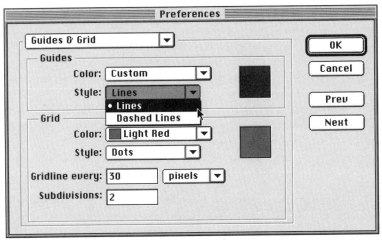

Figure 11-2. *You can customize the appearance of your guides and grids from Preferences with the Photoshop 4.0 Guides & Grids options*

Using guides and grids

Guides and grids are accessible from the View menu. To select display options, go to File: Preferences: Guides & Grids, shown in Figure 11-2. Here you will be able to choose the type of line as well as the color of the display line. For grids, you can also set the line spacing, in the Gridline Every field.

Guides have an advantage over grids, in that they can be moved, removed, or locked at any time. They also can be used selectively, reducing the distraction of a full-screen grid.

It's easy to work with guides:

- Drag from the horizontal ruler to create a horizontal guide, and drag from the vertical ruler to create a vertical guide.

- To move a guide, select the Move tool and drag it where you want it.

Guides can be used in conjunction with grids. A guide will also automatically align to a grid if you select View: Snap To Grid. To remove guides, drag the grid outside the image window. To clear all guides, choose View: Clear Guides. While grids will remain visible from file to file as long as Show Grid (View) is selected, guides appear only on the specific image file where they were created. When you save an image or graphic in any file format other than Photoshop, grids (and guides) will not be saved.

Redesigning with layers and grids

HotWired's award-winning redesign is built around rectilinear boxes where each box or series of adjacent boxes contains a color, text, or other graphical element. Anna McMillan—one of several HotWired designers—has done all the design and layout in Photoshop with guides that break the page into squares of 64 × 64 pixels, as shown in Figure 11-3.

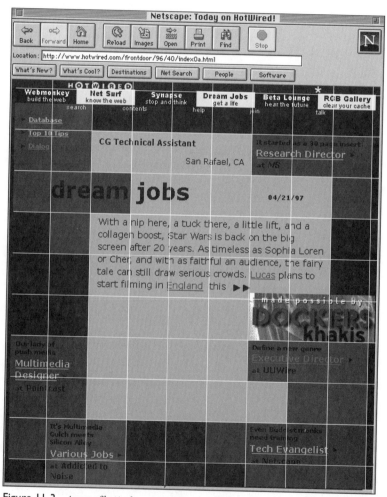

Figure 11-3. *Anna effectively uses guides to divide up her web page*

She actually works with Photoshop 3.05, creating her grids using a Photoshop plug-in called Grid Creator—available for free at *www.edesign.com/filters*. Grid Creator generates grids on any active layer in Photoshop. Shown in Figure 11-4, it's easy to use, but doesn't have Photoshop 4.0's snap-to features. (You can also create your own guides in other versions of Photoshop with channels and the drawing tools; see the sidebar "Creating guides with channels.")

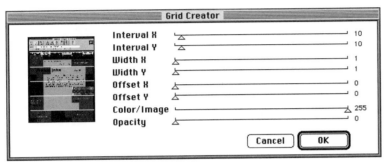

Figure 11-4. *The Grid Creator, a Photoshop plug-in, allows you to create grids in earlier versions of Photoshop*

Anna created the page shown in Figure 11-3 by first opening a 580 × 800-pixel Photoshop file containing a layer with a screenshot of the Netscape browser, and another layer containing the guides. Her first design pass was done mostly without color. She figured if it looked good in gray, it would look even better in color.

To see how the text would look, Anna cut actual HTML text from an HTML editor, clicked Photoshop's Type tool and then her image, and pasted the text. She kept her text options set at their default and chose aliased text. She knew that this would be only an approximation of how the text would ultimately look on a viewer's browser, but it gave her something to work with.

Part of the philosophy behind HotWired's redesign is to create pages that download quickly. This means less use of GIF and JPEG graphics and more emphasis on HTML text and color. Even so, for this page, Anna found herself working with many graphical elements. She placed each one in a separate Photoshop layer. (For other pages she has used as many as 100 layers.) When she was finished with the page, she printed a color copy that she sent along with the actual Photoshop file that went to a programmer. Then it was back to designing another HotWired page.

Animating your graphics with Actions

If you use animations in your web site—and nowadays, who doesn't?—you'll probably use Photoshop to create and prepare the graphics that make up the individual frames. Wouldn't it be nice if you could use Photoshop to actually see the animation in motion? Sean Parker of Option X nearly always includes an animated object in his web designs. To get a rough approximation of how the animation would look before actually building the animation in a GIF animation package, he used to place the sequence of images he wanted to animate into separate Photoshop layers and turn the Eye icons off and on.

With Photoshop 4.0, he discovered that he could create a Photoshop Action (Window: Show Actions) to simulate the animated look, freeing him of physically turning the Eye icons on and off. He finds it easier to design the web page when he knows how the animated object looks in the context of the rest of the static page. He finds his method especially useful when he wants to show a client an approximation of how the page will ultimately look.

Creating guides with channels

Besides using Grid Creator, you can create guides in other versions of Photoshop. You won't have the snap-to feature of Photoshop 4.0, but you will have a way to line up elements on a page.

Here is one way of creating guides using a separate Photoshop channel. You can get a similar result by using layers in versions of Photoshop 3.0 or higher:

1. Create a new channel, naming it *Guides*.

2. In the Channels palette's pop-up menu, select Options. In the Options dialog box, choose Color Indicates Selected Area and then choose an appropriate color for your lines. Dark lines are more visible on a light image and vice versa. Choose 65% opacity. Click OK.

3. Select the RGB channel and then turn on the Guide channel.

4. Open the Line Options palette (double-click on the Line tool in the Toolbar to open it) and set your line width to 1 or 2 pixels. Uncheck the Anti-aliased box. Since you are drawing straight lines, anti-aliasing isn't necessary. Set the Opacity to 100%.

5. With the foreground color set to black, draw the lines you want, both vertically and horizontally. Hold down the Shift key to constrain the line to the nearest 45-degree angle. To set the lines at precise *x* or *y* coordinates, use the Info palette.

This guide can be turned on and off as needed by clicking on the Guide channel's Eye icon. It can also be dragged and dropped into other images.

You'd think that it would be easy to simply create an Action that records layer Eye icons being turned on and off. But in reality, an Action will not register this procedure. What Sean has done instead is record the addition and subtraction of a layer mask. This results in a similar, layer-on and layer-off effect.

Figure 11-5 shows a single frame from one of Sean's animations that he created for the design firm of Porter/Novelle, which was part of the Japanese Automobile Manufacturers' industry web site.

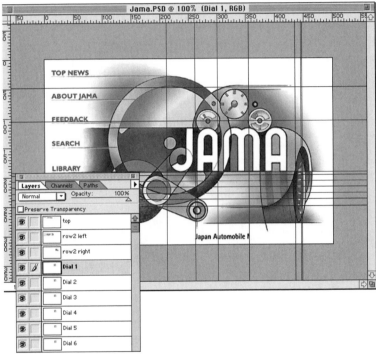

Figure 11-5. *Before Sean Parker built this animation in GifBuilder, he created a Photoshop Action that allowed him to preview the results directly in Photoshop*

This is how he animated his graphic using a Photoshop 4.0 action:

1. He created a new Action, named it *Flip Book,* and started recording.

2. Starting with the first animation layer, he selected Layers: Add Layer Mask: Hide All. He repeated this process for each successive animation layer. When a layer mask is applied, an additional thumbnail appears to the right of the layer thumbnail. Black indicates the entire layer is masked, or hidden. White indicates that the entire layer is visible. Layer masks can also control specific areas of a layer (of no value for our purpose here).

3. With the Action still recording, he went back to the first layer of the first frame of animation and selected Remove Layer Mask. (A dialog pops up and gives options to discard layer, apply layer, or cancel. Choose Discard, which then makes the contents of your layer visible.) He repeated this process for each successive layer in the animation. When he was finished, he stopped recording the Action.

Using guides to design and crop

After Gregg Hartling of Venu Interactive is finished designing and checking his web page in Photoshop 4.0, he uses guides and the snap-to feature to crop and save the various components.

Figure 11-6 shows the guides in place on one of Gregg's pages. Each component of the graphic is carefully grouped with another component, taking into consideration color palettes and final file size. In this example each component is saved as a GIF with its own Adaptive palette. By saving each graphic with its own optimized color palette, each component (especially the telephone with all its gradient colors) will display better at 16-bit or higher resolutions and degrade "gracefully" at 256 colors.

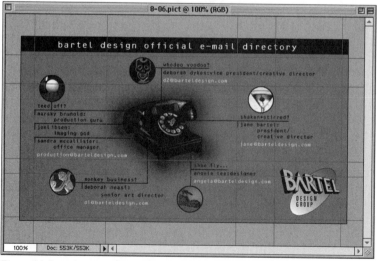

Figure 11-6. *Gregg Hartling uses Photoshop's Guides as crop marks*

To help him design his web pages, Gregg uses other Photoshop features, especially layers. He thinks of the live browser area as a "suitcase" where he needs to fit all the essential information (see Figure 11-7). Photoshop's layers assist him in the shuffling, grouping, and clustering of this information. Often his individual Photoshop files contain 15–30 layers.

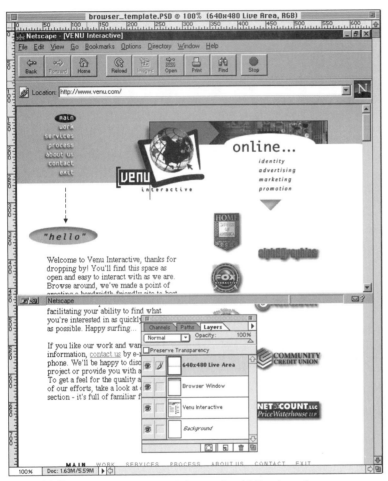

Figure 11-7. *Gregg uses layers to help him get the "fold" in his web pages*

Gregg always includes a layer containing a screenshot of Netscape 3.0 for Windows displayed on a 14-inch monitor, placing it above all the other layers. He places his design within the boundaries of this template, which is always visible. Since this template is 800 pixels long, he also includes another template in a second layer which shows him where the "fold" or bottom cut-off will appear, as shown in Figure 11-7. He clicks this layer off and on so he can see which part of his page will be visible without scrolling.

Like other designers profiled in this chapter, Gregg works with gray-scale graphics, not locking into any specific color palette until the end. By removing the complexity of color, he finds it easier to concentrate on shapes and context. When he is ready to add color, he clicks on Preserve Transparency in the Layers palette so he can selectively add color to each object in each layer.

Gregg has a good trick for getting an idea of how his text will look on a page: he imports the actual text from a browser to his Photoshop file. To do this, he follows these steps:

1. He determines the width of the text area within his Photoshop file.

2. Using an HTML editor, he codes the text into a table of the same width.

3. He opens the table in a browser and takes a screenshot.

4. He opens it in a new Photoshop file and deletes the white background with the Magic Wand set to zero tolerance and anti-aliasing turned off.

5. Then he runs a Photoshop Action that does the following:

    — Selects Similar (which takes care of the white inside the letters)

    — Deletes the selection (which gets rid of the all the white)

    — Inverts the selection (which selects just the text)

    — Copies the selection (which gets him ready to paste it into his current document)

Keeping boundaries with templates

Brian Frick of Discovery represents a new generation of web designers. He starts his design process in Illustrator, setting up the text. Illustrator gives him more control over the text than Photoshop does. When he is finished, he cuts and pastes the text into Photoshop, where he has gathered the other graphic elements to be used on the page.

Brian brings the text and graphical elements into a 609 × 1000 template he has created in Photoshop. This width assures that the page fits horizontally on the 640 × 480 pixel monitors typically used by most Discovery viewers. He uses the 1000-pixel length because Discovery has scrolling pages. At 340 pixels down, Brian has set a guideline, to remind him that most monitors will cut off at this point. When he designs a page, he tries to keep the most important elements of the page above this line, although sometimes, as a reminder to the viewer that the page actually scrolls, he places a graphic that straddles this line.

The template also contains generic ads, reminding Brian not to design in those areas. As he brings in the design elements, he adds guides as needed to align text and graphics. When he is finished, he adds more guides to help him crop, index, and separately save every element of the page.

In Figure 11-8, notice how he has created guides that show where he should crop. With the Crop tool, he cuts one section, then does a Save As. Then he reverts back to the original file (File: Revert), going through each square and repeating this process until he is finished.

Figure 11-8. *Brian uses guides to show where he should crop*

Working within the "live" area

After years of working with page layout programs, designer Barry Brooks of Surf Network finds himself thinking about pages differently and now uses Photoshop as his web layout tool of choice.

Since the pages that Barry designs vary from client to client, he doesn't use a standard web template. He places all the most important graphical elements, including navigation devices, the core ingredients, and main message, within a 640 × 480 pixel boundary, an area he refers to as "live." He lets other, nonessential elements bleed off the edge, as shown in Figure 11-9.

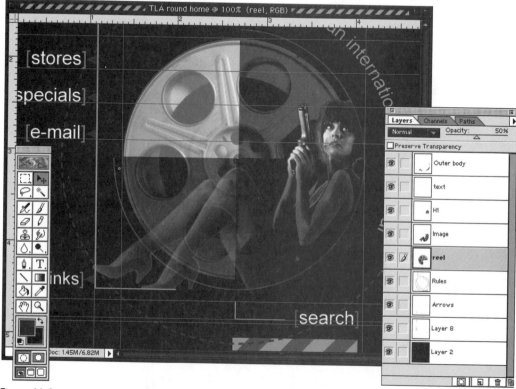

Figure 11-9. *Barry designs around a core 640 × 480 area*

Most of the time he uses a combination of grids and guides. With his grids at a value of 10 × 10 pixels, he sets the grid line preference to Dots so they are not as obtrusive. For emphasis, he uses guides that are solid lines and a different color than the grids, yet in contrast to the background color. For example, he places a guide to show where a marker or header goes.

While he designs, he turns both the guides and grids off to view his work clean. He uses dummy text and doesn't worry about leading or kerning since most of the text will be placed as HTML text anyway.

With Photoshop's Move tool, he moves graphics around, getting a feel for how they look. He also turns layers off and on. When he is finished, he makes a copy of the entire Photoshop file as "insurance protection" to prevent any loss or damage during the save and revert process. Then on the duplicate, he crops each graphical element out and saves it in either the GIF or JPEG format. He chooses Save a Copy so he can revert back to his original to pick another graphical element to save. Since he is well versed in HTML, he does all the coding himself, using the original Photoshop file as a reference.

Coding layout information in a layer

At MSNBC, the corroborative site of Microsoft and NBC, designers have discovered a way to streamline their web production process. Figure 11-10 shows a Photoshop file created by MSNBC designer Bobby Stevens, containing a wealth of layout and graphical data. Notice that the *guide* layer is separated from the background image containing the actual page by the *screen* layer, filled with white and set at 70% opacity. This allows parts of the finished page to show through. Because MSNBC programmers, (who actually do the coding and placing of the data on to the site) don't use Photoshop, the layers are merged and saved and either printed and given to them in hardcopy or as a file format they can open.

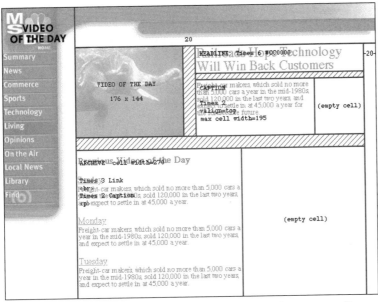

Figure 11-10. *Bobby contains page layout information in a layer to streamline the production process and make it easier to edit later*

In other large-scale web production environments we've seen, designers design the pages and then "hand off" the components of the page to a programmer who does the actual HTML (or other language) coding. Sometimes designers include an original Photoshop file along with their GIFs and JPEGs so the programmer can see how the elements relate to each other by viewing the layers. Other times a hardcopy composite is given instead of the Photoshop file. In either case, the programmer has to figure out the precise coordinates, color codes, etc. In many cases, this method works fine, but if there is a breakdown in communication between designer and programmer, or if time is limited, design nuances are lost.

Not only does MSNBC's method streamline the production process and make it less error-prone, but it gives the designer a handy reference guide that makes it easy to go back and make changes or update the page. It also makes it very easy for a designer to pass the work on to a fellow designer if need be. Granted, it takes work up front to calculate and enter all this data, but in many situations the payoff comes later, long after you've forgotten what color or font you used.

Unintended uses

When Photoshop was created so many years ago, surely no one imagined that one day it would be used like PageMaker or Quark Xpress as a layout tool. But as you've seen in this chapter, designers have discovered that when it comes to web work, it is the perfect layout tool. Not only does it give an accurate representation of how bitmap creations will look on the Web, but with layers it is easy to organize and store every graphical element imaginable. Will we ever completely mine the depths of this remarkable program?

THE PNG FORMAT

The Portable Network Graphic (PNG) format is a new file format developed as an alternative to GIF and JPEG, as mentioned in Chapter 4, *Creating GIFs from Scratch*. Support for PNG in the web community continues to grow. Microsoft Explorer 4.0 and Netscape Navigator 4.0.4 now both partially support PNG.

There are many advantages to using the PNG (pronounced "ping") format, including:

- 24-bit color support and lossless compression

- The ability to create and use up to 8-bit masks—thereby creating variable transparency

- Gamma controls, which give cross-platform consistency of image brightness

- A more sophisticated interlacing method that displays a preview of an image after only $1/64$th of the image has loaded, compared with GIF's preview after $1/8$th of an image has been loaded

In this appendix

- Creating PNG files in Photoshop 4.0

- Creating PNG transparency masks

- Making PNG graphics look the same on all systems

Creating PNG files in Photoshop 4.0

PNG is available as a file format option when you save a flattened RGB, grayscale, or indexed image. Figure A-1 shows the PNG dialog box.

Adam7 refers to the way PNG displays an image on a browser. If you choose this option, your PNG image will appear progressively on a web page, similar to the way an interlaced GIF appears, taking seven passes before the entire image appears instead of just a couple.

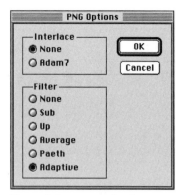

Figure A-1. *A screenshot from Photoshop 4.0 showing PNG options*

A PNG plug-in

You'll need Photoshop 4.0 or higher to create PNG files. However, Photoshop PNG plug-ins that support earlier versions of Photoshop for both the Mac and Windows are offered by InfinOp.

Microsoft Internet Explorer 4.0 and Netsape Navigator 4.04 both natively support PNG.

The other options allow you to choose the way that PNG applies its special "zlib" compression filters ("zlib"is the name of PNG's compression scheme). These five filters transform the image data losslessly so that it will compress better. If you choose None, all filtering is turned off, which usually results in a larger file size.

In theory, each of the five options will create a different file size, depending on the nature of your image. You'll have to experiment with your images to find the best setting, but keep in mind that there are only a few kilobytes, difference between the settings.

Creating PNG transparency masks

The PNG format supports up to an 8-bit alpha channel for RGB, grayscale, and indexed images. This means that masks can be created that contain smooth, gradual transitions between colors. In Figure C-87 you can see that regardless of the kind of background against which the images are placed, the image has a soft, glowing edge and the toucan's shadow blends seamlessly with the background. In Figure C-88, you can see that the shadow reacts differently depending on what image is underlying it. The result is a much more realistic effect than GIF transparency offers. (These images were created by Stefen Schneider.)

Creating variable transparency in RGB or grayscale mode is straightforward. You simply create a mask using one of several techniques and save the mask in the Channels palette. (Masks can be created using selections and the Quick Mask options; see *Chapter 5, Special Effects with Transparent GIFs*, for more on masks.) If you mask anti-aliased text, you won't get the halo or fringing effect that is so common with GIF89a masks. Keep in mind that an 8-bit mask increases your file size by at least 20%. (Also check to see if the current browsers support PNG's alpha channel feature. As of this writing, Netscape Navigator 4.04 does not support alpha channels and Internet Explorer only partially supports alpha channels. Check Greg Roelofs's PNG-Supporting Applications page at *www.cdrom.com/pub/png/pngapps.html.*)

What really increases file size, however, is using 32-bit RGB images instead of indexed images to create your PNGs. Indexed PNGs tend to be half the size of RGB PNGs. Unfortunately, Photoshop 4.0 can't save an indexed image containing an alpha channel in the PNG format. This is a bug in Photoshop's implementation of PNG, not a problem with the file format itself. Later versions of Photoshop will probably support indexed PNGs with an alpha channel, especially since this is a very important feature of the new format.

When Photoshop finally supports variable transparent masks with indexed images, they probably won't be easy to create. The reason is that many indexed images contain only a few colors. Unless you want to create a variable transparent mask that significantly adds to the file size of the image, you will need to use only the colors contained in the image. Even then, you will increase to the file size of an image. This is because you must still have separate palette entries for each level of transparency.

For instance, say you want to create variable transparency from a particular green in your image. Your palette will need to contain the original green as well as at least four other greens with different levels of transparency. The key will be to find the fewest colors needed that require different levels of transparency. (At some point you may decide that the 1-bit mask associated with GIF89a isn't so bad after all!)

Making PNG graphics look the same on all systems

Neither the JPEG nor the GIF file format contains gamma information specific to a particular image or the computer platform it was created on. This means that when an image is viewed on different systems it will probably look too light on one and too dark on another. When you save a file in the PNG format, however, gamma values specific to that image and system are saved. In theory, when a PNG image appears on another system, it self-corrects by comparing the gamma settings of the creator's system with the user's system. Because of this, it is very important that your system is properly calibrated and your gamma set properly. (See Chapter 4, *Creating GIFs from Scratch*, for information on setting your gamma.)

The alpha penalty

Since PNG compresses less than JPEG and since the alpha channel adds another 20% to the total file size, you'll want to work only with small images or graphics such as those associated with buttons and other graphical interface elements. You can use bigger images, of course, but you'll be losing out in the battle for smaller file sizes.

Archive with PNG

If you are not ready to include PNG with your web site, at least consider using the PNG format for archiving images. Unlike standard JPEG (even at its highest quality settings), saving, restoring, and re-saving a PNG image will not degrade its quality.

THIRD-PARTY SOFTWARE

For the typical user, Photoshop out of the box is good enough. You don't need anything else to create JPEGs and indexed GIFs, or to work with web-friendly colors and otherwise create web graphics. However, for web producers who want more control over what they do, the third party products featured here will be quite useful.

GIF creation

In general, I like the way Photoshop indexes color images in preparation for the GIF file format. I especially like the GIF89a Export Module included with later versions of Photoshop for creating transparent GIFs. However, there are a couple plug-ins that will give you more control over the indexing and dithering process.

HVS ColorGIF (Mac and Windows)

HVS ColorGIF from Digital Frontiers uses a patented "psycho-visual processing technique" that produces smaller GIF files than conventional dithering techniques such as those used by Photoshop. HVS Color also offers a high degree of user control over the color reduction process, including parameters such as gamma basic, thresholding and controlled weighting of color allocation, partition size, and set point that are not controllable in standard color reduction software.

As opposed to simple statistical methods, HVS tools are able to synthesize and allocate colors in a way that minimizes visible banding without having to resort to diffusion dithering. HVS Color images are comprised of regions of pure color. Because the resulting color structure is less complex, HVS Color images usually compress better than corresponding dithered images.

In this appendix

- GIF creation
- JPEG plug-ins
- Browser-safe color palettes
- Web-friendly Actions
- Kai's Power Tools
- Hybrid color makers
- Kodak Photo CD acquire module
- Vector to bitmap
- Debabelizer
- Resource fork stripper

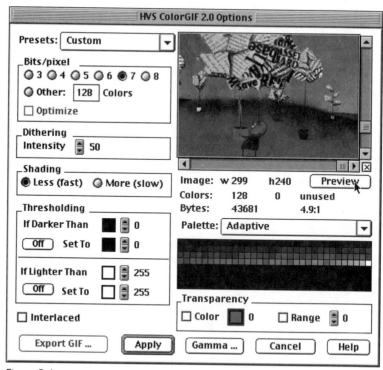

Figure B-1. *With HVS ColorGIF, you have both control and preview capabilities*

HVS Color also offers a preview mode so that you can see the effects of your choices before applying them, as that in Figure B-1.

> Digital Frontiers
> 1206 Sherman Ave.
> Evanston, IL 60202
> 800-328-7789
> 847-328-0880
> *www.digfrontiers.com*

PhotoGIF (Mac only)

PhotoGIF is a file-format plug-in that helps you create highly optimized, web-ready GIF images and animations from Photoshop. Like HVS ColorGIF, PhotoGIF offers more control and options than Photoshop and a preview mode so you can see the effects of your choices before you apply them. PhotoGIF requires Photoshop 3.0 or greater.

> Boxtop Software
> 101 N. Lafayette St.
> Starkville, MS 39759
> 601-324-1800
> *www.boxtopsoft.com*

JPEG plug-ins

While I have no gripe with the quality of the JPEGs that Photoshop creates, the user interface is weak. As it stands now, there is no real-time viewing of the effects of JPEG compression. You have to apply the compression, close the file, and then reopen it to see the effects. At least two plug-ins do better.

HVS JPEG (Mac and Windows)

In Chapter 6, *JPEG: All the Color You Want*, we discussed ways to optimize an image before applying JPEG compression. Essentially, this Photoshop plug-in does that for you automatically. You choose from a variety of optimizing algorithms (depending on the content of your image) and HVS JPEG does the rest. You can also see the effects in a preview window before actually applying the JPEG compression to your image.

> Digital Frontiers
> 1206 Sherman Ave.
> Evanston, IL 60202
> 800-328-7789
> 847-328-0880
> *www.digfrontiers.com*

ProJPEG

ProJPEG 2.1 is another Photoshop plug-in that provides capability for creating highly optimized, web-ready JPEG and progressive JPEG images. It also features a live image quality and file size preview that allows you to find the right file size to image quality ratio, as shown in Figure B-2.

> Boxtop Software
> 101 N. Lafayette St.
> Starkville, MS 39759
> 601-324-1800
> *www.boxtopsoft.com*

Browser-safe color palettes

Browser-safe palettes are included in later versions of Photoshop. However, if your version of Photoshop doesn't include one, you can either download one for free or buy a commercial product that will give you access to all the 216 browser-safe colors.

> *www.adobe.com/supportservice/custsupport/LIBRARY/2a7a.htm*

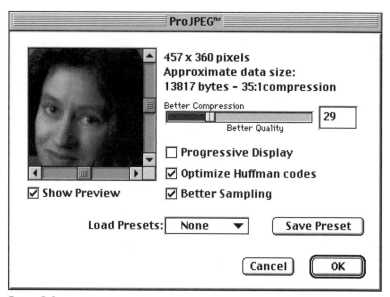

Figure B-2. *With the ProJPEG plug-in, you can see the effects of your compression in real-time and get an approximate idea of the file size*

Pantone ColorWeb (Mac only)

ColorWeb is a Pantone product that consists of a web-friendly Macintosh system-level color picker and a chromatically arranged printed source book (the Pantone Internet Color System Guide), which is in the familiar Pantone fan guide format.

Once loaded on to your system, the color picker is easily accessible from within Photoshop (or any other graphic program). The colors are arranged chromatically with Pantone-assigned numbers that can be cross-referenced with the source book. (The source book contains the Pantone reference numbers as well as the RGB and corresponding hexadecimal values.) ColorWeb suggests an alternative web-safe color, but you can choose any color you wish.

At first glance one wonders, why pay money for a web-safe palette? After all, web-safe palettes are widely available on the Net for free. Furthermore, with Apple's system 8.0, a web-safe palette is part of the Apple Color Picker. The real value of this product is the cross-reference with the source book. Anyone familiar with the Pantone fan format will find it easy to find the color they are looking for, access it by number in the color picker, and choose it. The guide is printed using Pantone's patented Hexachrome printing technology, so it is more accurate than traditionally printed swatches.

Pantone, Inc.
590 Commerce Blvd.
Carlstadt, NJ 07072
201-935-5500
www.pantone.com

Web-friendly Actions

Actions are easy to create on your own, but if someone else has
gone to all the work to create a useful one, why not use it? You have
a choice: shareware or a commercial product.

Photoshop Action Xchange

This is a free site for trading Actions.

jmc.mit.edu/photoshop/

KPT Actions

If you own Kai's Power Tools (listed next) and use Photoshop 4.0,
spend a few more dollars ($49.95 retail) and get KPT Actions, a
collection of 100 actions that will automatically create navigational
devices, text effects, and picture frames. If you take a moment and
watch each step of a particular Action, you'll also learn some valuable Photoshop techniques that you can apply to your own work.

MetaCreations
6303 Carpinteria Ave.
Carpinteria, CA 93013
805-566-6200
www.metacreations.com

Kai's Power Tools

Photoshop wouldn't be complete without a copy of Kai's Power
Tools. With these filters, you can create textures for backgrounds,
apply sophisticated blurring effects, spherize, and much, much more.

MetaCreations
6303 Carpinteria Ave.
Carpinteria, CA 93013
805-566-6200
www.metacreations.com

Hybrid color makers

In Chapter 4, *Creating GIFs from Scratch*, we showed you how to create your own browser-safe colors. If you don't want to go to the trouble of making your own, you can buy a couple products that will do most of the work for you.

DitherBox (Mac and Windows)

The DitherBox plug-in automatically convert any RGB color into a "web-safe" pattern (see Figure B-3). It also adjusts any hybrid color in real time. Change the color of a pixel and you'll instantly see how it affects the hybrid color. Create a collection of DitherBox hybrid colors, which you can use like solid colors. Paint and fill with DitherBox colors just as you would solid colors. Retail price is $29.95.

> RDG Tools
> 500 Benjamin Franklin Court
> San Mateo, CA 94401
> 800-451-3353
> *www.ditherbox.com*

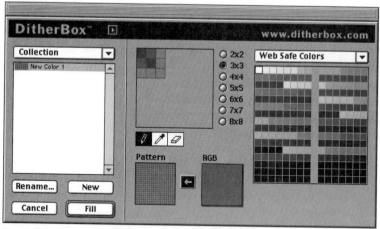

Figure B-3. *DitherBox automatically creates browser-safe colors from within Photoshop*

ColorSafe (Mac and Windows)

ColorSafe extends the 216-color web-safe palette to an almost infinite number of non-dithering hybrid colors and patterns. Download and try a functional demo at the Boxtop web site.

Boxtop Software
101 N. Lafayette St.
Starkville, MS 39759
601-324-1800
www.boxtopsoft.com

Kodak Photo CD acquire module

Many web producers rely on Kodak's Photo CD process to both archive and digitize images. In Chapter 2, *Improving Photos for the Web*, we showed you a way to use the Photoshop Photo CD Acquire module to do more than simply import your Photo CD images directly into Photoshop. If you download the proper module (Version 2.2 for the Macintosh, 1.0 for Windows) and open different gammas of the same image, you can actually improve tonal qualities of the image.

Photo CD digitizing services, by the way, are commonly available through local photo finishers and service bureaus. Kodak's web site has a list of service providers.

To download the Photo CD module:

www.kodak.com/productInfo/technicalInfo/
pcdAcquireModule.shtml

To find a Photo CD service near you:

www.kodak.com/digitalImaging/piwSites/piwSites.shtml

Vector to bitmap

If you want all the advantages of changeable type and vector drawing without the cost of buying Illustrator or Freehand, consider Human Software's Ottopaths, a Photoshop plug-in for both PC and Mac. Retail price is $99. With Ottpaths, you can create a path and wrap your text to that path without leaving Photoshop (see Figure B-4).

Human Software
P.O. Box 2280
Saratoga, CA 95070
408-399-0057
www.humansoftware.com

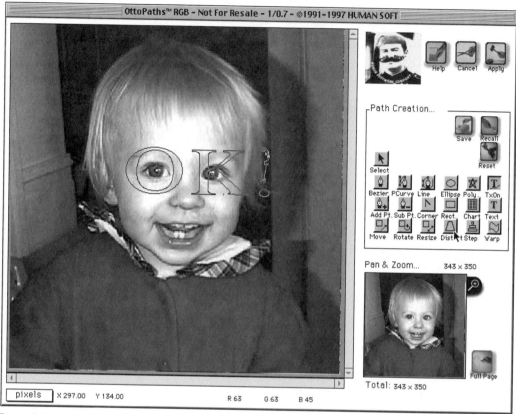

Figure B-4. *With Ottopaths, you can wrap text to a path and perform other tasks commonly done with a vector-based program such as Illustrator*

Debabelizer

Until Photoshop 4.0, I unequivocally recommended Debabelizer to all serious web producers. With 4.0's Actions, however, one of the most powerful features of Debabelizer, batch-processing, can be done with Photoshop as well. Still, this software tool is an important complement to Photoshop. It recognizes more file formats than Photoshop does, and its color reduction, scaling, and palette manipulating tools are arguably better than Photoshop's. Debabelizer is also very good at creating a "super" palette—a palette that contains colors optimized for series of similar images.

> Equilibrium
> 475 Gate Five Road, Suite 225
> Sausalito, CA 94965
> 415-332-4343
> *www.equilibrium.com*

Resource fork stripper

In Chapter 3, *Making Great GIFs*, we pointed out the difficulties in getting an accurate accounting of the true file size of your work. Using Boxtop Software's GIF Prep 1.0, a drag-and-drop utility, data from Macintosh graphics resource forks from GIF and JPEG files are eliminated to ensure that the file size you see in the Finder's Get Info dialog is accurate. You could always put your image on a server and get an accurate number that way, but using GIF Prep is much easier.

Boxtop Software
101 N. Lafayette St.
Starkville, MS 39759
601-324-1800
www.boxtopsoft.com

CONTRIBUTOR NOTES

Bill Atkinson designed software tools to empower creative people to express themselves. Now the marvelous software tools for digital photography on the Macintosh are empowering Bill to make beautiful color prints of his nature photographs. Whether making computers more humane and fun for people, or nourishing people's hearts with images of nature, Bill continues to share his life passions with all of us. He can be reached at *bill@natureimages.com* and *www.natureimages.com*.

Casey Caston is a web designer at c|net: The Computer Network (*www.cnet.com*), specializing in GIF animations and web-based advertising. He is also editor of the webzine "Fear Not Drowning" (*www.drowning.com*).

Ctein is a photographer, print maker, and author of *Post Exposure— Advanced Techniques for Photographic Printers* (Focal Press). He can be reached at *71246.216@compuserve.com* and *www.plaidworks.com/ctein/*.

Brian Frick worked for two years at Discovery Online before taking a job as a web designer at MSNBC in Seattle. His personal web site is located at *www.site2site.com/mogul/main.html*.

Bea Garcia is an art director at Savage Design Group, a leading graphic design firm in Houston, Texas. Before joining Savage, she was a designer in Dallas with Tom Hair Marketing Design. Bea designs print material, multimedia programs, and web sites for a myriad of clients and projects. The Savage Design Group web site can be viewed at *www.savagedesign.com*.

Chuck Green is an author and designer who heads Logic Arts, a design firm that specializes in creating templates for popular software programs. Chuck is the author of *The Desktop Publisher's Idea Book, 2nd Edition* (Random House), *Clip Art Crazy* (Peachpit Press), and is a regular contributor to numerous publications. You can reach him through his web site at *www.ideabook.com* or *chuckgreen@ideabook.com.*

Gregg Hartling is a designer at Venu Interactive, a Los Angeles–based creative agency specializing in interactive media. Its mission is to satisfy the growing demand for compelling, intelligent, and effective interactive design. Venu Interactive provides full-service advertising, marketing, and promotional services for high-profile corporate and entertainment industry clients. He can be contacted at *sales@venu.com* or *www.venu.com.*

John Hersey, based in Marin County, California, has created designs and illustrations for Swatch, *Wired,* Absolut, IBM, Apple, Adobe Systems, Microsoft, *The New York Times, The Los Angeles Times, The Washington Post,* and several national news magazines. In addition, he illustrated the covers of *GIF Animation Studio, Shockwave Studio,* and *Designing with JavaScript* (all from O'Reilly). A digital portfolio is available on his constantly changing web site at *www.hersey.com.* Contact him at *ultraduc@hersey.com.*

Corey Hitchcock, project web designer for The Gate (*www.sfgate.com*), in San Francisco, California, has an extensive background in design and illustration for print and multimedia and is now happily designing, animating, and slinging HTML on the Web for the Chronicle Publishing Company's web site.

Stephen Jablonsky is creative director and founder of Imaginary Studio, a digital design studio in New York City. He can be reached at *steve@imaginarystudio.com* and *www.imaginarystudio.com.*

Brad Johnson and **Julie Beeler** are partners in Second Story, a Portland, Oregon–based design studio specializing in entertainment-oriented interactive projects for clients including National Geographic, DreamWorks, NASA, Contax, and Yashica. They can be reached at *info@secondstory.com* and *www.secondstory.com.*

Luke Knowland is the former producer for HotWired's WebMonkey (*www.webmonkey.com*), and a founding member of the Humboldt Institute for Technological Studies (*www.hits.org*). He is presently living in Boston, Massachusetts. He can be contacted at *luke@hits.org* or *www.hits.org/hits/who/luke/.*

Steve Kruschwitz is a project webmaster at SFGate. He can be reached at *stevek@sfgate.com* or *www.sfgate.com.*

Anna McMillan is currently a designer at Wired Digital, where she works on web page design, animations, and illustration. She studied art and psychology at James Madison University in Harrisonburg, Virginia. She can be reached at *anna@wired.com.*

Sean Parker is the former animator and technical guru at Option X. He now is a principal in the multimedia company ParkerGrove in Washington, D.C. He can be reached at *spike@parkergrove.com* or *www.parkergrove.com.*

Stefan Schneider created the PNG images of toucans in Appendix A with LatinByrd software, created by his company Stefan Schneider Software, based in Vienna. He can be reached at *stefan@ping.at* or *members.ping.at/stefan/.*

Erika Sears is a full-time interactive media designer for Knowledge Adventure Software in Glendale, California. She received her BFA in Graphic Design and MFA in Computer Graphics/Interactive Media Design from the Rochester (NY) Institute of Technology. In addition to teaching, she has designed and developed a number of corporate and educational interactive media projects. She can be reached at *erikas@primenet.com* or *www.primenet.com/~erikas.*

Valerie Stambaugh is a designer based in Washington, D.C. She designed the author's site *www.cyberbohemia.com.* She can be reached at *valfrc@pipeline.com.*

Bobby Stevens has been a Photoshop user for six years. He started in print and moved to interactive CD-ROM and the Web two years ago. He has worked as a freelance graphic designer for clients like Seafirst, Adobe, and now MSNBC. He says his current passion is information design: "striving to find ways to help viewers navigate in this new and often confusing medium." His site is located at *www.halcyon.com/sdi/bobby.*

Johan Thorngren is a web designer at Icon Medialab in Madrid, Spain. In 1998, he plans on working at the Icon Medialab in San Francisco. He can be reached at: *johan.thorngren@iconmedialab.es.*

Turbo Ted is a new media artist residing in the California redwoods. He's working towards becoming a global telecommuter, living in various far flung corners of the globe while working with people anywhere via satellite. He can be reached at *shag@sirius.com* and *www.sirius.com/~shag.*

Judd Vetrone, formerly of HotWired, is currently a freelance illustrator, concentrating on illustration and animation for the web. He also works at Process39, a company specializing in multimedia design. He can be reached at *judd@netjet.com.*

Tom Walker is a New York designer and web producer. He can be reached at *tkwalker@interport.net*.

James Yang is New York–based illustrator with such clients as *The New Yorker, The New York Times*, and *Forbes*. He can be reached at *JamesY2200@aol.com*.

Maria Yap is the founder and production director of Option X–based in Capitola, California. She can be reached at *MariaYap@aol.com*.

Mikkel Aaland is a photographer, writer, web producer, and author of six books, including *Sweat* (1978), *County Fair Portraits* (1981), *Digital Photography* (1992), *Still Images in Multimedia* (1996), *Photoshop for the Web* (1998), and *The Sword of Heaven* (not yet published). He has contributed both text and/or photography to *Wired*, *Digital Creativity*, *Pre*, *American Photo*, *Newsweek*, *Graphis*, *Publish*, and *MacWeek*, as well as several European publications. His photography has been exhibited in major institutions around the world, including the Bibliotheque Nationale in Paris and the former Lenin Museum in Prague. He is the recipient of the National Art Directors award for photography. Aaland is also the co-founder of Tor Productions, a multimedia company founded in 1989 and based in San Francisco, specializing in the use of the still image in new media. He has lectured and taught on that subject at Stanford University, Drexel University, and the University of California at Berkeley, as well as at computer graphics conferences around the country.

Our look is the result of reader comments, our own experimentation, and feedback from distribution channels. Distinctive covers complement our distinctive approach to technical topics, breathing personality and life into potentially dry subjects.

The animal on the cover of *Photoshop for the Web* is an Amazon parrot, also known as a blunt-tailed parrot. There are over 320 species of parrots, all of them easily distinguishable from other species of birds because of their large, hooked bills and their feet, on which the first and fourth toes are reversed, creating a pincer that aids in climbing trees. Most parrots also use their beaks to help in climbing.

There are 26 species and 52 subspecies of blunt-tailed parrots. These birds are mostly green, with bright coloring on their heads, wings, or elsewhere. The names of the subspecies tend to be descriptive: blue-fronted parrot, yellow-headed parrot, orange-winged amazon parrot. As their natural habitat is thickly grown forests, blunt-tailed parrots are excellent climbers, but awkward at flying and walking. In captivity, they often stop flying altogether.

Parrots were among the first domesticated animals. A helmsman of Alexander the Great was the first to bring live parrots to Europe. One reason for their popularity as pets is their ability to mimic human speech. Parrots have never been observed displaying this ability in the wild. They are naturally intelligent and gregarious, and it is believed that when they are kept in solitary cages they learn to mimic sounds as a way of entertaining themselves.

Legend has it that Christopher Columbus saw a flock of parrots in the air and they prompted him to change his course, thus discovering America.

Nancy Priest designed the interior book layout for FrameMaker and the color insert layout in QuarkXPress 3.32. Edie Freedman designed the cover of this book, using a 19th-century engraving from the Dover Pictorial Archive. The cover layout was produced with QuarkXPress 3.32, using the Gill Sans Condensed and Garamond Light Italic fonts.

Mike Sierra implemented the interior layout in FrameMaker 5.0. The illustrations that appear in the book were prepared by Robert Romano in Photoshop 4.0 and Macromedia Freehand 7.0. This colophon was written by Clairemarie Fisher O'Leary.

Whenever possible, our books use a durable and flexible lay-flat binding. If the page count exceeds the lay-flat binding's limit, perfect binding is used.

More Titles from O'Reilly

Designing Web Content

Designing with JavaScript

By Nick Heinle
1st Edition September 1997
256 pages, Includes CD-ROM
ISBN 1-56592-300-6

Written by the author of the "JavaScript Tip of the Week" web site, this new Web Review Studio book focuses on the most useful and applicable scripts for making truly interactive, engaging web sites. You'll not only have quick access to the scripts you need, you'll finally understand why the scripts work, how to alter the scripts to get the effects you want, and, ultimately, how to write your own groundbreaking scripts from scratch.

GIF Animation Studio

By Richard Koman
1st Edition October 1996
184 pages, Includes CD-ROM
ISBN 1-56592-230-1

GIF animation is bringing the Web to life— without plug-ins, Java programming, or expensive authoring tools. This book details the major GIF animation programs, profiles work by leading designers (including John Hersey, Razorfish, Henrik Drescher, and Erik Josowitz), and documents advanced animation techniques. A CD-ROM includes freeware and shareware authoring programs, demo versions of commercial software, and the actual animation files described in the book. *GIF Animation Studio* is the first release in the new Web Review Studio series.

Shockwave Studio

By Bob Schmitt
1st Edition March 1997
200 pages, Includes CD-ROM
ISBN 1-56592-231-X

This book, the second title in the new Web Review Studio series, shows how to create compelling and functional Shockwave movies for web sites. The author focuses on actual Shockwave movies, showing how the movies were created. The book takes users from creating simple time-based Shockwave animations through writing complex logical operations that take full advantage of Director's power. The CD-ROM includes a demo version of Director and other software sample files.

Photoshop for the Web

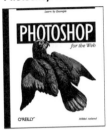

By Mikkel Aaland
1st Edition April 1998
248 pages, ISBN 1-56592-350-2

Photoshop for the Web shows you how to use the world's most popular imaging software to create Web graphics and images that look great and download blazingly fast. The book is crammed full of step-by-step examples and real-world solutions from some of the country's hottest Web producers, including *HotWired, c\net, Discovery Online, Second Story, SFGate*, and more than 20 others.

Designing with Animation

By J. Scott Hamlin
1st Edition June 1998 (est.)
250 pages (est.), ISBN 1-56592-441-X

Designing with Animation treats the subject of Web animation with a level of sophistication that both meets the needs of today's demanding professionals and pushes the envelope for amateur animators. Topics include GIF animation, advanced animation techniques, seamless integration of animation, creative interactive animation with Java, JavaScript, and Macromedia Flash, vector-based and 3D animation, adding sound to animation, and animation techniques with Photoshop.

Web Navigation: Designing the User Experience

By Jennifer Fleming
1st Edition March 1998 (est.)
250 pages (est.), Includes CD-ROM
ISBN 1-56592-351-0

Web Navigation: Designing the User Experience offers the first in-depth look at designing web site navigation. Through case studies and designer interviews, a variety of approaches to navigation issues are explored. The book focuses on designing by purpose, with chapters on entertainment, shopping, identity, learning, information, and community sites. The accompanying CD-ROM includes a tour of selected sites, a "netography," and trial versions of popular software tools.

O'REILLY™

TO ORDER: **800-998-9938** • *order@oreilly.com* • *http://www.oreilly.com/*
OUR PRODUCTS ARE AVAILABLE AT A BOOKSTORE OR SOFTWARE STORE NEAR YOU.
FOR INFORMATION: **800-998-9938** • **707-829-0515** • *info@oreilly.com*

Developing Web Content

WebMaster in a Nutshell, Deluxe Edition

By O'Reilly & Associates, Inc.
1st Edition September 1997
374 pages, includes CD-ROM & book
ISBN 1-56592-305-7

The Deluxe Edition of *WebMaster in a Nutshell* is a complete library for web programmers. It features the Web Developer's Library, a CD-ROM containing the electronic text of five popular O'Reilly titles: *HTML: The Definitive Guide*, 2nd Edition; *JavaScript: The Definitive Guide*, 2nd Edition; *CGI Programming on the World Wide Web*; *Programming Perl*, 2nd Edition—the classic "camel book"; and *WebMaster in a Nutshell*, which is also included in a companion desktop edition.

HTML: The Definitive Guide, 2nd Edition

By Chuck Musciano & Bill Kennedy
2nd Edition May 1997
552 pages, ISBN 1-56592-235-2

This complete guide is chock full of examples, sample code, and practical, hands-on advice to help you create truly effective web pages and master advanced features. Learn how to insert images and other multimedia elements, create useful links and searchable documents, use Netscape extensions, design great forms, and lots more. The second edition covers the most up-to-date version of the HTML standard (HTML version 3.2), Netscape 4.0 and Internet Explorer 3.0, plus all the common extensions.

Dynamic HTML: The Complete Reference

By Danny Goodman
1st Edition June 1998 (est.)
1000 pages (est.), ISBN 1-56592-494-0

Dynamic HTML: The Complete Reference is an indispensable compendium for Web content developers. It contains complete reference material for all of the HTML tags, CSS style attributes, browser document objects, and JavaScript objects supported by the various standards and the latest versions of Netscape Navigator and Microsoft Internet Explorer.

Frontier: The Definitive Guide

By Matt Neuburg
1st Edition February 1998
618 pages, 1-56592-383-9

This definitive guide is the first book devoted exclusively to teaching and documenting Userland Frontier, a powerful scripting environment for web site management and system level scripting. Packed with examples, advice, tricks, and tips, Frontier: The Definitive Guide teaches you Frontier from the ground up. Learn how to automate repetitive processes, control remote computers across a network, beef up your web site by generating hundreds of related web pages automatically, and more. Covers Frontier 4.2.3 for the Macintosh.

WebMaster in a Nutshell

By Stephen Spainhour & Valerie Quercia
1st Edition October 1996
374 pages, ISBN 1-56592-229-8

Web content providers and administrators have many sources for information, both in print and online. WebMaster in a Nutshell puts it all together in one slim volume for easy desktop access. This quick reference covers HTML, CGI, JavaScript, Perl, HTTP, and server configuration.

Designing for the Web: Getting Started in a New Medium

By Jennifer Niederst
with Edie Freedman
1st Edition April 1996
180 pages, ISBN 1-56592-165-8

Designing for the Web gives you the basics you need to hit the ground running. Although geared toward designers, it covers information and techniques useful to anyone who wants to put graphics online. It explains how to work with HTML documents from a designer's point of view, outlines special problems with presenting information online, and walks through incorporating images into web pages, with emphasis on resolution and improving efficiency.

O'REILLY™

TO ORDER: **800-998-9938** • *order@oreilly.com* • *http://www.oreilly.com/*
OUR PRODUCTS ARE AVAILABLE AT A BOOKSTORE OR SOFTWARE STORE NEAR YOU.
FOR INFORMATION: **800-998-9938** • **707-829-0515** • *info@oreilly.com*

Developing Web Content

CGI Programming on the World Wide Web

By Shishir Gundavaram
1st Edition March 1996
450 pages, ISBN 1-56592-168-2

This book offers a comprehensive explanation of CGI and related techniques for people who hold on to the dream of providing their own information servers on the Web. It starts at the beginning, explaining the value of CGI and how it works, then moves swiftly into the subtle details of programming.

Information Architecture for the World Wide Web

By Louis Rosenfeld & Peter Morville
1st Edition January 1998
226 pages, ISBN 1-56592-282-4

Learn how to merge aesthetics and mechanics to design web sites that "work." This book shows how to apply principles of architecture and library science to design cohesive web sites and intranets that are easy to use, manage, and expand. Covers building complex sites, hierarchy design and organization, and techniques to make your site easier to search. For webmasters, designers, and administrators.

Learning VBScript

By Paul Lomax
1st Edition July 1997
616 pages, includes CD-ROM
ISBN 1-56592-247-6

This definitive guide shows web developers how to take full advantage of client-side scripting with the VBScript language. In addition to basic language features, it covers the Internet Explorer object model and discusses techniques for client-side scripting, like adding ActiveX controls to a web page or validating data before sending it to the server. Includes CD-ROM with over 170 code samples.

Web Client Programming with Perl

By Clinton Wong
1st Edition March 1997
228 pages, ISBN 1-56592-214-X

Web Client Programming with Perl shows you how to extend scripting skills to the Web. This book teaches you the basics of how browsers communicate with servers and how to write your own customized web clients to automate common tasks. It is intended for those who are motivated to develop software that offers a more flexible and dynamic response than a standard web browser.

JavaScript: The Definitive Guide, 3rd Edition

By David Flanagan & Dan Shafer
3rd Edition June 1998 (est.)
800 pages (est.), ISBN 1-56592-392-8

This third edition of the definitive reference to JavaScript covers the latest version of the language, JavaScript 1.2, as supported by Netscape Navigator 4.0. JavaScript, which is being standardized under the name ECMAScript, is a scripting language that can be embedded directly in HTML to give web pages programming-language capabilities.

O'REILLY™

TO ORDER: **800-998-9938** • *order@oreilly.com* • *http://www.oreilly.com/*

OUR PRODUCTS ARE AVAILABLE AT A BOOKSTORE OR SOFTWARE STORE NEAR YOU.

FOR INFORMATION: **800-998-9938** • **707-829-0515** • *info@oreilly.com*

Graphics/Multimedia

Encyclopedia of Graphics File Formats, 2nd Edition

By James D. Murray & William vanRyper
2nd Edition May 1996
1154 pages, Includes CD-ROM
ISBN 1-56592-161-5

The second edition of the *Encyclopedia of Graphics File Formats* provides the convenience of quick look-up on CD-ROM, up-to-date information through links to the World Wide Web, as well as a printed book—all in one package. Includes technical details on more than 100 file formats. The CD-ROM includes vendor file format specs, graphics test images, coding examples, and graphics conversion and manipulation software. An indispensable online resource for graphics programmers, service bureaus, and graphic artists.

Director in a Nutshell

By Bruce A. Epstein
1st Edition May 1998 (est.)
450 pages (est.), ISBN 1-56592-382-0

Director in a Nutshell is the most concise and complete guide available for Director® and its powerful scripting language, Lingo. The reader gets both the nitty-gritty details and the bigger context in which to use the multiple facets of Director. It is a high-end handbook, at a low-end price—an indispensable desktop reference that every Director user wants and needs.

Photoshop in a Nutshell

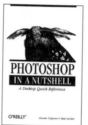

By Donnie O'Quinn & Matt LeClair
1st Edition October 1997
610 pages, ISBN 1-56592-313-8

Photoshop 4's powerful features make it the software standard for desktop image design and production. But they also make it an extremely complex product. This detailed reference defines and describes every tool, command, palette, and sub-menu of Photoshop 4 to help users understand design options, make informed choices, and reduce time spent learning by trial-and-error.

QuarkXPress in a Nutshell

By Donnie O'Quinn
1st Edition May 1998 (est.)
350 pages (est.), ISBN 1-56592-399-5

This quick reference describes every tool, command, palette, and sub-menu in QuarkXPress 4, providing users with a detailed understanding of the software so they can make informed choices and reduce time spent learning by trial-and-error.

O'REILLY™

TO ORDER: **800-998-9938** • *order@oreilly.com* • *http://www.oreilly.com/*
OUR PRODUCTS ARE AVAILABLE AT A BOOKSTORE OR SOFTWARE STORE NEAR YOU.
FOR INFORMATION: **800-998-9938** • **707-829-0515** • *info@oreilly.com*

Internet for Everyone

The Whole Internet User's Guide & Catalog

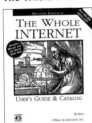

By Ed Krol
2nd Edition April 1994
574 pages, ISBN 1-56592-063-5

Still the best book on the Internet. This is the second edition of our comprehensive introduction to the Internet. An international network that includes virtually every major computer site in the world, the Internet is a resource of almost unimaginable wealth. In addition to the World Wide Web, electronic mail, and news services, thousands of public archives, databases, and other special services are available. This book covers Internet basics—like email, file transfer, remote login, and network news. Useful to beginners and veterans alike, also includes a pull-out quick-reference card.

The Whole Internet for Windows 95

By Ed Krol & Paula Ferguson
1st Edition October 1995
650 pages, ISBN 1-56592-155-0

The Whole Internet for Windows 95, the most comprehensive introduction to the Internet available today, shows you how to take advantage of the vast resources of the Internet with Microsoft Internet Explorer, Netscape Navigator, Microsoft Exchange, and many of the best free software programs available from the Net. Also includes an introduction to multimedia for PCs and a catalog of interesting sites to explore.

AOL in a Nutshell

By Curt Degenhart & Jen Muehlbauer
1st Edition June 1998 (est.)
512 pages (est.), ISBN 1-56592-424-X

This definitive reference breaks through the hype and shows advanced AOL users and sophisticated beginners how to get the most out of AOL's tools and features. You'll learn how to customize AOL so it works the way you want it to, work around annoying idiosyncrasies, avoid unwanted email and Instant Messages, understand Parental Controls, and turn off intrusive advertisements. It's an indispensable guide for users who aren't dummies.

Bandits on the Information Superhighway

By Daniel J. Barrett
1st Edition February 1996
246 pages, ISBN 1-56592-156-9

Most people on the Internet behave honestly, but there are always some troublemakers. *Bandits* provides a crash course in Internet "street smarts," describing practical risks that every user should know about. Filled with anecdotes, technical tips, and the advice of experts from diverse fields, *Bandits* helps you identify and avoid risks online, so you can have a more productive and enjoyable time on the Internet.

Smileys

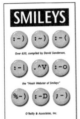

By David W. Sanderson
1st Edition March 1993
93 pages, ISBN 1-56592-041-4

From the people who put an armadillo on the cover of a system administrator book comes this collection of the computer underground hieroglyphs called "smileys." Originally inserted into email messages to denote "said with a cynical smile" :-) , smileys now run rampant throughout the electronic mail culture. They include references to politics 7:^] (Ronald Reagan), entertainment C]:-= (Charlie Chaplin), history 4:-) (George Washington), and mythology @-) (cyclops). They can laugh out loud %-(I) wink ;-) yell :- (0) frown :-(and even drool :-)~

Internet in a Nutshell

By Valerie Quercia
1st Edition October 1997
450 pages, ISBN 1-56592-323-5

Internet in a Nutshell is a quick-moving guide that goes beyond the "hype" and right to the heart of the matter: how to get the Internet to work for you. This is a second-generation Internet book for readers who have already taken a spin around the Net and now want to learn the shortcuts.

O'REILLY™

TO ORDER: **800-998-9938** • *order@oreilly.com* • *http://www.oreilly.com/*
OUR PRODUCTS ARE AVAILABLE AT A BOOKSTORE OR SOFTWARE STORE NEAR YOU.
FOR INFORMATION: **800-998-9938** • **707-829-0515** • *info@oreilly.com*

Perl

Perl Resource Kit—UNIX Edition

By Larry Wall, Nate Patwardhan, Ellen Siever,
David Futato & Brian Jepson
1st Edition November 1997
1812 pages, ISBN 1-56592-370-7

The *Perl Resource Kit—UNIX Edition* gives you the most comprehensive collection of Perl documentation and commercially enhanced software tools available today. Developed in association with Larry Wall, the creator of Perl, it's the definitive Perl distribution for webmasters, programmers, and system administrators.

The *Perl Resource Kit* provides:

- Over 1800 pages of tutorial and in-depth reference documentation for Perl utilities and extensions, in 4 volumes.
- A CD-ROM containing the complete Perl distribution, plus hundreds of freeware Perl extensions and utilities—a complete snapshot of the Comprehensive Perl Archive Network (CPAN)—as well as new software written by Larry Wall just for the Kit.

Perl Software Tools All on One Convenient CD-ROM

Experienced Perl hackers know when to create their own, and when they can find what they need on CPAN. Now all the power of CPAN—and more—is at your fingertips. *The Perl Resource Kit* includes:

- A complete snapshot of CPAN, with an install program for Solaris and Linux that ensures that all necessary modules are installed together. Also includes an easy-to-use search tool and a web-aware interface that allows you to get the latest version of each module.
- A new Java/Perl interface that allows programmers to write Java classes with Perl implementations. This new tool was written specially for the Kit by Larry Wall.

Experience the power of Perl modules in areas such as CGI, web spidering, database interfaces, managing mail and USENET news, user interfaces, security, graphics, math and statistics, and much more.

Perl in a Nutshell

By Stephen Spainhour, Ellen Siever & Nathan Patwardhan
1st Edition July 1998 (est.)
600 pages (est.), ISBN 1-56592-286-7

The perfect companion for working programmers, *Perl in a Nutshell* is a comprehensive reference guide to the world of Perl. It contains everything you need to know for all but the most obscure Perl questions. This wealth of information is packed into an efficient, extraordinarily usable format.

Programming Perl, 2nd Edition

By Larry Wall, Tom Christiansen & Randal L. Schwartz
2nd Edition September 1996
670 pages, ISBN 1-56592-149-6

Coauthored by Larry Wall, the creator of Perl, the second edition of this authoritative guide contains a full explanation of Perl version 5.003 features. It covers Perl language and syntax, functions, library modules, references, and object-oriented features, and also explores invocation options, debugging, common mistakes, and much more.

Perl 5 Desktop Reference

By Johan Vromans
1st Edition February 1996
46 pages, ISBN 1-56592-187-9

This is the standard quick-reference guide for the Perl programming language. It provides a complete overview of the language, from variables to input and output, from flow control to regular expressions, from functions to document formats—all packed into a convenient, carry-around booklet. Updated to cover Perl version 5.003.

Learning Perl, 2nd Edition

By Randal L. Schwartz & Tom Christiansen
Foreword by Larry Wall
2nd Edition July 1997
302 pages, ISBN 1-56592-284-0

In this update of a bestseller, two leading Perl trainers teach you to use the most universal scripting language in the age of the World Wide Web. Now current for Perl version 5.004, this hands-on tutorial includes a lengthy new chapter on CGI programming, while touching also on the use of library modules, references, and Perl's object-oriented constructs.

O'REILLY™

TO ORDER: **800-998-9938** • *order@oreilly.com* • *http://www.oreilly.com/*
OUR PRODUCTS ARE AVAILABLE AT A BOOKSTORE OR SOFTWARE STORE NEAR YOU.
FOR INFORMATION: **800-998-9938** • **707-829-0515** • *info@oreilly.com*

Perl

Advanced Perl Programming

By Sriram Srinivasan
1st Edition August 1997
434 pages, ISBN 1-56592-220-4

This book covers complex techniques for managing production-ready Perl programs and explains methods for manipulating data and objects that may have looked like magic before. It gives you necessary background for dealing with networks, databases, and GUIs, and includes a discussion of internals to help you program more efficiently and embed Perl within C or C within Perl.

Learning Perl on Win32 Systems

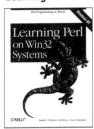

By Randal L. Schwartz, Erik Olson & Tom Christiansen
1st Edition August 1997
306 pages, ISBN 1-56592-324-3

In this carefully paced course, leading Perl trainers and a Windows NT practitioner teach you to program in the language that promises to emerge as the scripting language of choice on NT. Based on the "llama" book, this book features tips for PC users and new NT-specific examples, along with a foreword by Larry Wall, the creator of Perl, and Dick Hardt, the creator of Perl for Win32.

Mastering Regular Expressions

By Jeffrey E. F. Friedl
1st Edition January 1997
368 pages, ISBN 1-56592-257-3

Regular expressions, a powerful tool for manipulating text and data, are found in scripting languages, editors, programming environments, and specialized tools. In this book, author Jeffrey Friedl leads you through the steps of crafting a regular expression that gets the job done. He examines a variety of tools and uses them in an extensive array of examples, with a major focus on Perl.

The Perl Cookbook

By Tom Christiansen & Nathan Torkington
1st Edition June 1998 (est.)
600 pages (est.), ISBN 1-56592-243-3

This collection of problems, solutions, and examples for anyone programming in Perl covers everything from beginner questions to techniques that even the most experienced Perl programmers might learn from. It contains hundreds of Perl "recipes," including recipes for parsing strings, doing matrix multiplication, working with arrays and hashes, and performing complex regular expressions.

O'REILLY™

TO ORDER: **800-998-9938** • **order@oreilly.com** • **http://www.oreilly.com/**
OUR PRODUCTS ARE AVAILABLE AT A BOOKSTORE OR SOFTWARE STORE NEAR YOU.
FOR INFORMATION: **800-998-9938** • **707-829-0515** • **info@oreilly.com**

How to stay in touch with O'Reilly

1. Visit Our Award-Winning Web Site

http://www.oreilly.com/

★ "Top 100 Sites on the Web" —*PC Magazine*
★ "Top 5% Web sites" —*Point Communications*
★ "3-Star site" —*The McKinley Group*

Our web site contains a library of comprehensive product information (including book excerpts and tables of contents), downloadable software, background articles, interviews with technology leaders, links to relevant sites, book cover art, and more. File us in your Bookmarks or Hotlist!

2. Join Our Email Mailing Lists

New Product Releases
To receive automatic email with brief descriptions of all new O'Reilly products as they are released, send email to:
listproc@online.oreilly.com
Put the following information in the first line of your message (*not in* the Subject field):
subscribe oreilly-news

O'Reilly Events
If you'd also like us to send information about trade show events, special promotions, and other O'Reilly events, send email to:
listproc@online.oreilly.com
Put the following information in the first line of your message (*not in* the Subject field):
subscribe oreilly-events

3. Get Examples from Our Books via FTP

There are two ways to access an archive of example files from our books:

Regular FTP
- ftp to:
  ftp.oreilly.com
  (login: anonymous
  password: your email address)
- Point your web browser to:
  ftp://ftp.oreilly.com/

FTPMAIL
- Send an email message to:
  ftpmail@online.oreilly.com
  (Write "help" in the message body)

4. Contact Us via Email

order@oreilly.com
To place a book or software order online. Good for North American and international customers.

subscriptions@oreilly.com
To place an order for any of our newsletters or periodicals.

books@oreilly.com
General questions about any of our books.

software@oreilly.com
For general questions and product information about our software. Check out O'Reilly Software Online at **http://software.oreilly.com/** for software and technical support information. Registered O'Reilly software users send your questions to: **website-support@oreilly.com**

cs@oreilly.com
For answers to problems regarding your order or our products.

booktech@oreilly.com
For book content technical questions or corrections.

proposals@oreilly.com
To submit new book or software proposals to our editors and product managers.

international@oreilly.com
For information about our international distributors or translation queries. For a list of our distributors outside of North America check out:
http://www.oreilly.com/www/order/country.html

O'Reilly & Associates, Inc.
101 Morris Street, Sebastopol, CA 95472 USA
TEL 707-829-0515 or 800-998-9938
(6am to 5pm PST)
FAX 707-829-0104

O'REILLY™

Titles from O'Reilly

International Distributors

UK, EUROPE, MIDDLE EAST AND NORTHERN AFRICA (EXCEPT FRANCE, GERMANY, SWITZERLAND, & AUSTRIA)

INQUIRIES
International Thomson Publishing Europe
Berkshire House
168-173 High Holborn
London WC1V 7AA
United Kingdom
Telephone: 44-171-497-1422
Fax: 44-171-497-1426
Email: itpint@itps.co.uk

ORDERS
International Thomson Publishing Services, Ltd.
Cheriton House, North Way
Andover, Hampshire SP10 5BE
United Kingdom
Telephone: 44-264-342-832 (UK)
Telephone: 44-264-342-806 (outside UK)
Fax: 44-264-364418 (UK)
Fax: 44-264-342761 (outside UK)
UK & Eire orders: itpuk@itps.co.uk
International orders: itpint@itps.co.uk

FRANCE

Editions Eyrolles
61 bd Saint-Germain
75240 Paris Cedex 05
France
Fax: 33-01-44-41-11-44

FRENCH LANGUAGE BOOKS
All countries except Canada
Telephone: 33-01-44-41-46-16
Email: geodif@eyrolles.com
English language books
Telephone: 33-01-44-41-11-87
Email: distribution@eyrolles.com

GERMANY, SWITZERLAND, AND AUSTRIA

INQUIRIES
O'Reilly Verlag
Balthasarstr. 81
D-50670 Köln
Germany
Telephone: 49-221-97-31-60-0
Fax: 49-221-97-31-60-8
Email: anfragen@oreilly.de

ORDERS
International Thomson Publishing
Königswinterer Straße 418
53227 Bonn, Germany
Telephone: 49-228-97024 0
Fax: 49-228-441342
Email: order@oreilly.de

JAPAN

O'Reilly Japan, Inc.
Kiyoshige Building 2F
12-Banchi, Sanei-cho
Shinjuku-ku
Tokyo 160-0008 Japan
Telephone: 81-3-3356-5227
Fax: 81-3-3356-5261
Email: kenji@oreilly.com

INDIA

Computer Bookshop (India) PVT. Ltd.
190 Dr. D.N. Road, Fort
Bombay 400 001 India
Telephone: 91-22-207-0989
Fax: 91-22-262-3551
Email: cbsbom@giasbm01.vsnl.net.in

HONG KONG

City Discount Subscription Service Ltd.
Unit D, 3rd Floor, Yan's Tower
27 Wong Chuk Hang Road
Aberdeen, Hong Kong
Telephone: 852-2580-3539
Fax: 852-2580-6463
Email: citydis@ppn.com.hk

KOREA

Hanbit Media, Inc.
Sonyoung Bldg. 202
Yeksam-dong 736-36
Kangnam-ku
Seoul, Korea
Telephone: 822-554-9610
Fax: 822-556-0363
Email: hant93@chollian.dacom.co.kr

SINGAPORE, MALAYSIA, AND THAILAND

Addison Wesley Longman Singapore PTE Ltd.
25 First Lok Yang Road
Singapore 629734
Telephone: 65-268-2666
Fax: 65-268-7023
Email: daniel@longman.com.sg

PHILIPPINES

Mutual Books, Inc.
429-D Shaw Boulevard
Mandaluyong City, Metro
Manila, Philippines
Telephone: 632-725-7538
Fax: 632-721-3056
Email: mbikikog@mnl.sequel.net

CHINA

Ron's DataCom Co., Ltd.
79 Dongwu Avenue
Dongxihu District
Wuhan 430040
China
Telephone: 86-27-3892568
Fax: 86-27-3222108
Email: hongfeng@public.wh.hb.cn

ALL OTHER ASIAN COUNTRIES

O'Reilly & Associates, Inc.
101 Morris Street
Sebastopol, CA 95472 USA
Telephone: 707-829-0515
Fax: 707-829-0104
Email: order@oreilly.com

AUSTRALIA

WoodsLane Pty. Ltd.
7/5 Vuko Place, Warriewood NSW 2102
P.O. Box 935
Mona Vale NSW 2103
Australia
Telephone: 61-2-9970-5111
Fax: 61-2-9970-5002
Email: info@woodslane.com.au

NEW ZEALAND

Woodslane New Zealand Ltd.
21 Cooks Street (P.O. Box 575)
Waganui, New Zealand
Telephone: 64-6-347-6543
Fax: 64-6-345-4840
Email: info@woodslane.com.au

THE AMERICAS

McGraw-Hill Interamericana Editores, S.A. de C.V.
Cedro No. 512
Col. Atlampa 06450
Mexico, D.F.
Telephone: 52-5-541-3155
Fax: 52-5-541-4913
Email: mcgraw-hill@infosel.net.mx

SOUTH AFRICA

International Thomson Publishing South Africa
Building 18, Constantia Park
138 Sixteenth Road
P.O. Box 2459
Halfway House, 1685 South Africa
Telephone: 27-11-805-4819
Fax: 27-11-805-3648